GOOD COOKING FOR TWO

CAVENDISH HOUSE

CONTENTS

Key to Symbols
This is a guide to each recipe's preparation and cooking

☆ Easy

☆ ☆ Requires special care

☆ ☆ ☆ Complicated

This is a guide to the cost of each dish and will, of course, vary according to region and season

① Inexpensive

① ① Reasonable

① ① ① Expensive

This is a guide to the preparation and cooking time required for each dish and will vary according to the skill of the individual cook

⊠ Less than 1 hour

⊠ ⊠ Between 1 hour and 2½ hours

⊠ ⊠ ⊠ Over 2½ hours

Recipes by Isabel James
Editor: Philippa Davenport
Art Editor: Andrzej Bielecki
Assistant Art Editor: Janet Sayer
Photographer: Paul Kemp
Stylist: Sue Lacey
Food prepared for photography by Elaine Bastable
Illustrations by Jannat Houston

Published by
Marshall Cavendish Books Limited
58 Old Compton Street
London W1V 5PA

© Marshall Cavendish Limited 1973 – 84

ISBN 0 85685 900 1

Printed and bound in Italy by New Interlitho SpA.

INTRODUCTION

Most people have to cook for two sometimes—whether they're newly-weds, flat-sharing friends, parents of young children or a retired couple—and yet most recipes are geared to four, six or more servings and are often almost impossible to reduce. (How can you divide one egg white by three?) Here are recipes specifically designed for the person who is cooking for two, likes good food but resents the waste of over-buying. All our recipes are for two and there are menus to suit all sorts of occasions. Here are delicious recipes for the shoe-string cook; a special occasion menu for when you want to splash out; we show you how to cook a whole meal in one pot; offer time-saving dishes to cook the day before; cosy suppers on a tray. We suggest a variety of appetizers; special ways to cheer up vegetables; and a selection of mouth-watering fruits and desserts; we show you how to make a joint, turkey or duck economically and deliciously provide two or three different meals for two.

And, equally important, here too are lots of useful hints and ideas to help you organize your kitchen and budget for two with minimum wastage; what quantities to buy and how to plan your menus; how to store food and what equipment you will need.

SHOPPING AND COOKING FOR TWO

How many times have you tried to cook a meal for two, only to find that every recipe you read is intended for four, or even six, people? It is extremely frustrating to have to halve, quarter or even 'third' the ingredients listed, and of course, such things as '3 eggs' resolutely refuse to be divided! And yet, when you come to think of it, some of the most important meals in the world are just for two people: the relaxing dinner for mum and dad when the children have gone to bed; everyday meals for the older or retired couple; Sunday lunch for the newlyweds; or even that palpitating first (and *very* important) meal for the new boyfriend.

Recipes for all occasions

It is for these and many other occasions that *Cooking for Two* has been specially devised. Here are recipes for all contingencies, from the panic-stricken emergency to the long-planned special occasion. Here also are suggestions to make the routine everyday choices a bit more exciting and varied. If you envy the range of materials and scope of recipes available to large families or more ambitious hostesses, read on and discover that the more intimate meals you require need not be restricted or predictable.

Planning

There's no getting away from it. Before you can embark on a successful career of cooking for two, you must reconcile yourself to the fact that economical *and* imaginative meals call for a higher degree of organization in the kitchen. You need to know which items can profitably be bought in bulk, and which ones can't; which foods keep and for how long; how to create different dishes from the same basics; how to put the leftovers from one meal to good use in another. Native ingenuity will help you solve some of the problems as they come up, of

course. But you can in fact avoid most of them entirely by common sense. And that means planning your meals more than one day ahead—preferably for the whole week, if you have to go out to work during the day and your shopping time is limited.

An economic roasting joint

Take meat for example. Many families of two don't ever have a roast —simply because it is not worth buying a large and costly joint of good roasting meat just for two people. Or is it? Maybe we can learn something here from our ancestors whose vast joints served the entire family from Sunday to Friday inclusive, like the old recipe for Vicarage Mutton: hot on Sunday, cold on Monday, hashed on Tuesday, minced on Wednesday, curried on Thursday, and broth on Friday!
Even with modern refrigeration that's asking a bit much for two people. All the same, there are many splendid recipes that call for cooked meat—as you'll see from this book. So why not have a proper roast on Sunday and get at least two more imaginative meals from the same joint. This, of course, will justify the cost of the meat in the first place: in fact, it's just as economic as buying three separate smaller items.

Cooking ahead

Equally important for the busy cook are the advantages of cooking ahead. To prepare two or three casseroles or cook-ahead dishes at the same time actually takes little more time than preparing one. And, of course, some casseroles and curries improve with keeping for a day or so and then being re-heated. And at the same time rather than simply throwing away the bones of the joint or feeding them to a friendly dog, it calls for very little effort and even less time to put them into a stockpot with a few leftover (or fresh) vegetables and some seasoning

to make a fine rich stock.With the advent of instant stock cubes, this culinary art is dying out—sadly, because nothing can really replace a true homemade stock. But to deny yourselves this luxury because there are only two of you would be a total surrender to 'convenience' cooking.

Buying

Luckily canned foods, and to a large extent, packet foods, come in varying sizes. It would be foolish to buy a large can of fruit, for example, when a smaller one would be more sensible. There is nothing worse than having half a tin of peaches or tomatoes mouldering in valuable refrigerator space until it simply *has* to be thrown away. However, even for two, buying in bulk can save money with some items. Good olive oil works out much cheaper (about half price in some cases) if bought in half or one gallon cans. And if kept in a cool, dark place it will keep in indefinitely.
There are some things which self-evidently should *not* be bought in large quantities: eggs, coffee (which rapidly loses its fragrance even in bean form) and salad vegetables, about which more later. On the other hand, rice, cereals, flour, sugar and pasta are worthwhile bought in bulk, and should be stored in airtight tins or glass jars. And if you're cooking with wine—and propose to drink some with the meal as well—it makes more sense to buy one of the litre bottles which most shippers are putting on the market nowadays. Use it for both cooking and drinking. Very often the litre bottles come with plastic fitted caps and, once opened, will keep adequately for 2-3 days.

Storing

Naturally, in the end the quantities of food you can buy depend on how long they will keep and what storage facilities you have at your disposal. If you are the proud owner of a deep-freeze, you have few problems. However, a large freezing compartment in the refrigerator is quite suitable for two—but do take proper notice of the maker's recommended storage times for frozen foods.

With fresh foods, there are very few that come naturally in quantities which relate to two people. One lettuce, for example, might be too much for two on one day; therefore it needs to be stored in an airtight plastic container in the bottom of the refrigerator. (This is where your shopping must be geared to your planning—you should really plan for salad on consecutive days, not a week ahead, though obviously there's no need to settle for the same kind of salad two days running.) To help you avoid overstocking—which may well be your biggest single source of waste—here is a list of the average storage times of major items.

Meat

All meat should be put into the refrigerator, after being wiped and wrapped in foil, immediately after you get home from shopping. Joints will keep up to 5 days, steaks and chops rather less, bacon slightly longer. Cooked meat will also keep from 3-5 days if kept in an airtight container.

Fish

Fish should be eaten as fresh as possible, and whether cooked or uncooked, within 2 days at the most. For frozen fish, consult the star ratings on the refrigerator, and keep in the freezing compartment.

Poultry

Fresh poultry, drawn and wrapped in foil will keep up to three days, as will cooked birds if placed in the refrigerator as soon as they have cooled. Frozen ducks, chicken etc. should be kept wrapped, in the freezer, or for not more than 2 days in the main body of the refrigerator.

Vegetables

Salad vegetables such as lettuce will keep up to 4 or 5 days in an airtight container in the bottom of the refrigerator. Greens will stay fresh for up to a week in the vegetable compartment. For frozen vegetables, follow the manufacturer's instructions.

Cheese

Hard cheeses are best stored in the main body of the refrigerator, wrapped in foil, but they should be taken out a couple of hours before use. Soft cheeses should only be bought as and when required.

Eggs

Eggs should not be kept in the refrigerator. Keep them in a cool dark cupboard for up to a fortnight, if they were fresh when bought. Whole yolks can be covered with water and will keep adequately for 2 or 3 days, and egg whites will last up to 4 days in an airtight container.

Herbs and spices

It is of course, impossible and unnecessary to buy spices in very minute quantities. A basic spice rack of ground spices (cinnamon, cloves, coriander, cumin, paprika, turmeric etc.) is a good investment, however many people you have to cook for. But certain spices, like nutmeg, are best bought whole and grated as required—and that applies especially to pepper which rapidly loses its fragrance and aroma unless bought as whole peppercorns and ground from a pepper mill.

In season, it is a good idea to have your own fresh herbs growing in the kitchen or in a window box. Mint, parsley and chives are particularly useful and their growth will just keep pace with the requirements of cooking for two.

Equipment

Finally a word about kitchen equipment, which is so much more important than many people think. In order to cook well you must have the basic tools available, otherwise everything will be twice as hard and take up so much more precious time. First and foremost, every cook needs a good set of knives—the carbonated steel ones are the best and sharpest—and to begin with you should have at least three of varying length. To keep them sharp, use an ordinary butcher's steel or sharpening stone. Next on the list is a palette knife, a fish slice, a long-handled spoon for basting, a perforated draining spoon, and of course a set of wooden spoons. For whisking egg whites, nothing does the job better than a balloon whisk, and for other whisking chores a rotary whisk or an electric hand whisk are ideal. A chopping board is important because if you chop things on other surfaces you ruin both your knives and the surfaces. Every kitchen should have a lemon squeezer, a four-sided grater, a sieve and a colander for draining vegetables. Other items of great priority are weighing scales and a measuring jug—trying to guess what a specified amount say, of flour, looks like is sheer misery when you are in a hurry.

Obviously you need the usual complement of saucepans (with well-fitting lids), meat tins and baking tins, plus a small oven-proof *gratin* dish and a casserole. But if you're fortunate to have collected all these things already—then the one luxury item on this list of essentials has to be a blender—invaluable for puréeing and making soups.

BREAKFAST

Breakfast can be one of the most pleasant meals to share, and it seems a pity not to get up just a little earlier to enjoy the pleasures of a leisurely breakfast together.

Bacon and Mushroom Scramble

Preparation and cooking time:
15 minutes
This is a basic scramble recipe. Bacon and mushroom is a traditional combination, but you can vary it according to what is available—tomatoes, chopped peppers, onion, kidney, flaked smoked haddock or chicken livers can make a nice change.

3 bacon slices
40 g/1½ oz butter
5 ml/1 teaspoon cooking oil
50 g/2 oz mushrooms
2 eggs
salt
freshly ground black pepper

Fry the bacon in 25 g/1 oz of butter and the oil until crisp. Remove from the pan, chop into small pieces and keep warm.
Slice the mushrooms and fry them for a few minutes, then transfer them to the bacon dish.
Melt the remaining butter in a thick bottomed saucepan without browning. Whisk the eggs in a bowl and pour them in to the saucepan. Stir continuously with a wooden spoon over medium heat, allowing the eggs to cook without sticking to the bottom or sides of the pan.

Opposite: Country breakfast with Homemade Muesli and Toasted Oatcakes with Bacon and Apple

When the egg is three-quarters cooked, remove the pan from the heat, add the fat from the frying pan and continue stirring away from the heat until all liquid is absorbed and the eggs are soft and glossy. Then fold in the bacon and mushrooms, season to taste with salt and pepper, and serve immediately on hot buttered toast.

Toasted Oatcakes with Bacon and Apple

Preparation and cooking time:
30 minutes
Oatcakes have been eaten in Britain for centuries. Here is a savoury version with bacon and apple topping but they are delicious served with grilled halved tomatoes and sausages, or spread with creamy butter and marmalade or homemade preserves.

75 g/3 oz medium-ground
    oatmeal
25 g/1 oz wholemeal flour
1.25 ml/¼ teaspoon salt
15 g/½ oz butter
15 ml/1 tablespoon boiling
    water
4 bacon slices, crisply fried
4 apple rings, fried

Heat the oven to 350°F (Gas Mark 4 180°C).
Put the oatmeal, flour and salt in a mixing bowl and rub together thoroughly. Melt the butter in a small pan over low heat without browning.
Make a well in the centre of the oatmeal mixture, pour the melted butter into it and start to mix in with a fork. Add a tablespoon of boiling water and continue mixing to dough consistency with lightly floured hands.
Sprinkle a little flour and oatmeal

on to a pastry-board. Roll out the dough to 1 cm/¼ in thickness and cut into rounds with a 6.5 cm/2 in diameter pastry cutter. Lift the oatcakes on to a lightly-greased baking-sheet and bake on the top shelf of the oven for 20 minutes.
Serve the cooked oatcakes topped with crisp bacon, fried apple rings and mustard or a sharp pickle.

Homemade Muesli

Preparation time:
15 minutes—plus 8 hours
Many shops now sell various brands of ready made muesli, but it really is a lot nicer when prepared at home, using fresh ingredients. This version—with dried apricots—can be made all the year round but, of course, you can vary the fruits according to season and availability. And you can experiment with different nuts, as well.

30 ml/2 tablespoons medium-ground
    oatmeal
50 g/2 oz dried apricots
1 red dessert apple
the juice of half a lemon
60 ml/4 tablespoons soft brown sugar
5 ml/1 teaspoon ground cinnamon
100 g/4 oz chopped walnuts
150 ml/5 fl oz natural yogurt

Soak the oatmeal overnight in 150 ml/¼ pint of water. Put the apricots in a separate bowl, cover with water and also leave to soak overnight.
Next morning drain the apricots, pat them dry with absorbent kitchen paper chop roughly and add them to the soaked oatmeal.
Core and roughly chop the apple (leaving on the skins,) and toss in lemon juice. Stir in to the oatmeal and apricot mixture. Sprinkle on first the brown sugar, then the cinnamon and finally the coarsely chopped walnuts.
Serve with fresh yogurt.

5

LIGHT LUNCHES

Here are recipes specifically designed for those who plan to eat their main meal in the evening, and want something nutritious but simple at midday. The dishes can be eaten at home, of course, or made up into lunch boxes to eat on a journey or, for the working couple, they make an appetizing alternative to café sandwiches or canteen food. Simply wrap the food in aluminium foil, add a paper napkin and a piece of fruit or some salad vegetables, and you have a perfectly balanced packed meal. It can be unwrapped without fuss in a car or train, carried into the park for a fresh air lunch break, or eaten in the office if the weather turns nasty.

Tortilla

Preparation and cooking time:
20 minutes
This is a huge, flat Spanish-style omelette—a meal on its own. A single one is enough for two people and the fillings can be varied. The version given here is sometimes called a tortilla Castellana.

10 ml/2 teaspoons olive oil
15 ml/1 tablespoon butter
1 large onion, chopped
4 medium-sized potatoes, cooked and diced
15 ml/1 tablespoon chopped parsley
4 large eggs, lightly beaten
salt
freshly ground black pepper

Melt the oil and butter in 20 cm/8 in frying pan. Fry the onion gently for 10 minutes, or until almost cooked. Add the diced potato and heat through stirring now and then. Then add the parsley.
Season the eggs with salt and freshly

ground black pepper to taste. Turn the heat up high, pour the egg mixture into the pan and quickly reduce the heat to moderate. Run a palette knife round the edge and shake the pan to avoid sticking. Lift the omelette slightly with the palette knife and, when cooked and golden underneath, slide it out onto a warm plate then return to the pan to cook the reverse side. Serve cold.

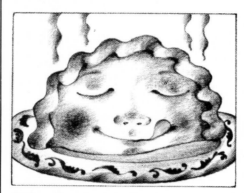

Homemade Cornish Pasties

Preparation and cooking time: *1¼ hours*
This homemade version of the famous English classic is a pleasant treat and equally good hot or cold.

225 g/8 oz sirloin steak
1 medium-sized onion, chopped
1 medium-sized potato, diced
salt
freshly ground black pepper
7.5 ml/1½ teaspoons dried mixed herbs
225 g/8 oz shortcrust pastry
1 egg, beaten

Heat the oven to 425°F (Gas Mark 7, 220°C).
Cut the steak into very small pieces and mix in the onion and potato. Season with salt, freshly ground black pepper and mixed herbs.
Divide the pastry into 2 and on a floured board roll out each piece into a 20 cm/8 in round. Place half the meat mixture into the centre of each pastry round. Dampen the edges of the pastry with a little water and

draw them together in the centre, sealing well. Flute the edges and brush all over with the beaten egg. *Place* the pasties on a baking tray and bake for 15 minutes, then reduce heat to 350°F (Gas Mark 4, 180°C) and cook for a further 40 minutes.

Meat Loaf

Preparation and cooking time:
1¼ hours
This meat loaf can be served hot with homemade tomato sauce (basic recipe) for a light lunch, or it is just as good served cold cut into thick slices for a packed lunch-box. It could even be sliced and put into sandwiches. This recipe will provide enough for two meals.

450 g/1 lb lean minced beef
225 g/8 oz pork sausage meat
2 large onions, minced
1 garlic clove, crushed
5 ml/1 teaspoon dried mixed herbs
salt
freshly ground black pepper
2 slices bread
30 ml/2 tablespoons milk
1 egg, beaten

Heat the oven to 375°F (Gas Mark 5, 190°C).
Put the lean minced beef into a large mixing-bowl. Add the sausage meat, minced onions, garlic, herbs and a good seasoning of salt and freshly ground black pepper.
Remove the crust from the bread and soak the slices in the milk. Squeezing out the excess milk, add the bread to the rest of the ingredients, and mix everything together as thoroughly and evenly as possible. Then add the beaten egg and bind the mixture together.
Press the mixture into a 1 kg/2 lb loaf tin and bake for 1¼ hours.

Opposite: Take Homemade Cornish Pasties and Meat Loaf for a packed lunch. Inset: Tortilla

INSTANT DINNERS

Florentine Plaice Fillets

Preparation and cooking time:
25 minutes
Here is an instant freezer meal, but do remember to remove the packages from the freezer in good time, so that they are thoroughly defrosted before you start cooking.

175 g/6 oz frozen chopped spinach
salt
freshly ground black pepper
175 g/8 oz frozen plaice fillets
150 ml/5 fl oz instant cheese sauce
   (from a packet or basic recipe)
freshly ground nutmeg
15 ml/1 tablespoon double
   cream
40 g/1½ oz Cheddar cheese,
   grated
15 ml/1 tablespoon breadcrumbs
15 g/½ oz butter

Heat the oven to 350°F (Gas Mark 4, 180°C).
Butter a shallow baking dish and place the spinach in it. Season with salt and freshly ground black pepper. Arrange the fish fillets on top of the spinach and season again.
Make up the cheese sauce according to the instructions on the packet and add a few good gratings of nutmeg. Pour the sauce over the fish and sprinkle the grated cheese and breadcrumbs on top.
Dot with flecks of butter and bake on the top shelf of the oven for 20 minutes.

Instant Chilli con Carne

Preparation and cooking time:
15-20 minutes
This one really is absolutely instant but, on days when you have a little more time to spare, you can make it even nicer by using freshly cooked minced beef.

25 g/1 oz butter
1 medium-sized onion, chopped
1 small red pepper, chopped
425 g/15 oz canned savoury minced
   steak
425 g/15 oz canned red kidney beans
15 ml/1 tablespoon tomato purée
10 ml/2 teaspoons chilli con carne
   seasoning (or powdered chilli)
salt
freshly ground black pepper

Melt the butter and fry the chopped onion and pepper in it until soft (about 10-15 minutes).
Add the savoury minced steak, the drained kidney beans, tomato purée and chilli powder. Season with salt and pepper. Stir thoroughly and heat through.
Serve with crusty bread and butter, and a side salad.

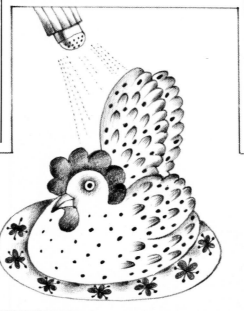

Chicken Veronique

Preparation and cooking time:
30 minutes
Here is a very handy recipe for jazzing-up shop bought, pre-cooked chicken pieces. When you get the chicken home, remove all the skin, discard it, then separate the flesh from the bones.

300 ml/10 fl oz canned condensed
   chicken soup
50 ml/2 fl oz dry white wine
2 large cooked chicken breasts
salt
freshly ground black pepper
30 ml/2 tablespoons double
   cream
100 g/4 oz white grapes, halved and
   seeded

In a large saucepan bring the condensed soup and white wine to simmering point. Strain the liquid into a clean saucepan, add the chicken and simmer very gently for 20-25 minutes until the chicken is thoroughly heated through.
Meanwhile, heat the grill
Remove the saucepan from the heat, season, stir in the cream and grapes and pour the mixture into an ovenproof serving dish. Cook under the hot grill until the sauce begins to bubble.
Serve with tinned new potatoes and a side salad.

Opposite: When you're in a hurry, try Chicken Veronique, with grapes, wine and a quick, creamy sauce.

ONE-POT CASSEROLES

Casseroling is a miraculous way of cooking: cheap, tough cuts of meat are transformed into mouth-watering gourmet treats. Slow, moist cooking tenderizes the meat (and all the nutrients are captured in the gravy) but, although cooking time is lengthy, not much work is required of the cook.

Traditional Irish Stew with Parsley Dumplings *(see left)*

☆　　①　　✕ ✕ ✕

Preparation and cooking time: $2\frac{3}{4}$ hours
On a cold and frosty day it is hard to beat an Irish Stew. It's so easy to prepare and very warming—all you need is a large cooking pot and some big soup-plates to serve it in.

1 kg/2 lb middle neck and scrag end of lamb, mixed
30 ml/2 tablespoons flour, seasoned with salt and pepper
2 large onions, sliced
225 g/8 oz potatoes, cut into chunks
15 ml/1 tablespoon pearl barley
25 ml/½ teaspoon mixed herbs
425 ml/15 fl oz boiling water
For the parsley dumplings:
50 g/2 oz shredded suet
100 g/4 oz self-raising flour
15 ml/1 tablespoon chopped parsley
salt
freshly ground black pepper

Toss the pieces of lamb in the seasoned flour, then put them into a saucepan together with the sliced onion, potatoes and pearl barley. Sprinkle on the mixed herbs and another good seasoning of salt and freshly ground black pepper.
Pour on the boiling water and bring to the boil. Remove any scum that may have formed on top. Reduce the heat, cover the saucepan with a lid and simmer very gently for 2½ hours.
To make the dumplings, mix the suet, flour and parsley together, add pepper and salt and enough water to make a fairly elastic dough. Divide the dough into 4, and roll each piece into a round.
20-25 minutes before the end of cooking time check that the stew is on the boil, and drop the dumplings into the pan. Replace the lid and finish cooking at boiling point.
Serve immediately with buttered carrots if extra vegetables are required.

Simple Strogonoff

☆　　① ①　　✕ ✕

Preparation and cooking time:
2-2¼ hours
The classic version of Filet de Boeuf Strogonoff is made with tiny strips of fillet steak, sautéed and served in sour cream sauce. This variation, although made with a cheaper cut of meat, is just as exciting.

450g/1 lb lean chuck steak
15 ml/1 tablespoon seasoned flour
a little dripping or cooking oil
1 medium-sized onion, chopped
5 ml/1 teaspoon tomato purée
150 ml/5 fl oz canned condensed mushroom soup
50 ml/2 fl oz natural yogurt
salt
freshly ground black pepper

Heat oven to 300°F (Gas Mark 1-2, 150°C).
Cut the meat into bite-sized chunks and toss in the seasoned flour.
Heat some dripping (or cooking oil) in a thick-bottomed saucepan, and fry the meat to brown nicely. Add the onion and continue to cook for 1-2 minutes. Then stir in the tomato purée, add the soup and yogurt and season with a little more pepper and salt.
Stir thoroughly, place the lid on the saucepan and simmer very gently on top of the stove—or in a low oven—for 1½-2 hours, or until the meat is tender.

Veal Marengo

☆　　① ①　　✕ ✕

Preparation and cooking time:
$1\frac{1}{4}$ hours
Being left with only one saucepan after a battle, Napoleon's chef improvised this garnish—originally for chicken, but it goes just as well with veal. There is no need for this dish to be expensive if you ask your butcher to sell you cut-up pie or stewing veal.

25 g/1 oz butter
1 large onion, sliced
450 g/1 lb lean veal, cubed
1 small green pepper, chopped
7.5 ml/1½ teaspoons flour
2.5 ml/½ teaspoon of dried mixed herbs
1 garlic glove, crushed
30 ml/2 tablespoons tomato purée
150 ml/5 fl oz dry white wine
50 ml/2 fl oz good stock (basic recipe)
salt
freshly ground black pepper
Heat the oven to 350°F (Gas Mark 4, 180°C).
Melt the butter in a thick-bottomed pan and gently fry the onion until it has turned pale gold. Then add the veal and brown very lightly. Next add the chopped pepper and allow that to fry for 1-2 minutes.
Stir in the flour, followed by the herbs and garlic. Add the tomato purée, and finally the wine and stock.
Stir well. Season to taste with salt and freshly ground black pepper. Place the lid on the casserole and cook in the oven for 1 hour.

DEAD-BROKE DINNERS

This is the section to read, and here are the recipes to follow when your funds are very low, or when you want to cut down on housekeeping expenses because you're saving up for something special like a holiday.

Contrary to popular belief, there is no reason why lack of money has to restrict you to a mundane diet, or prevents you from eating very tasty and nutritious foods. Even meat like lamb need not be beyond your budget. Select a cheap cut and

carefully cook it with aromatic herbs to make it really inviting. Enjoy the challenge, experiment with foods and cooking methods that may be new to you, and see just what delicious dishes you can conjure from a shoestring budget.

Ragout of Mutton

Preparation and cooking time:
2¼ hours

1 kg/2 lb scrag end or middle neck of
    mutton or lamb
salt and freshly ground black pepper
15 ml/1 tablespoon mutton dripping
2 medium-sized onions, roughly
    chopped
1 garlic clove, chopped
5 ml/1 teaspoon mixed herbs
1 bay leaf
15 ml/1 tablespoon flour
300 ml/10 fl oz boiling water
6 small new potatoes, scrubbed
2 medium-sized tomatoes

Heat the oven to 315°F (Gas Mark 3½,
157°C).
Season the pieces of meat with salt
and freshly ground pepper, then fry
them in the dripping. When browned
turn the meat into a casserole.
Fry the onions and garlic for a few
minutes, then add them to the meat
and sprinkle on the mixed herbs.
To the remaining juices in the pan
add the flour and stir over low heat
until smooth. Then add the boiling
water, in a slow trickle, stirring all
the time until you have a smooth
gravy. When it reaches boiling-point
pour the gravy over the meat.
Cover the casserole with a well fitting
lid and cook in the oven for 1 hour.
Then add the potatoes and tomatoes
and cook for a further hour.
Taste to check the seasoning and serve
with a green vegetable.

Curried Eggs

 ① ⊠

Preparation and cooking time:
50 minutes

50 g/2 oz butter
1 small onion, chopped
1 small cooking apple, peeled and
    chopped
10 ml/2 teaspoons curry powder
1.25 ml/¼ teaspoon ground turmeric
1.25 ml/¼ teaspoon ground ginger
40 g/1½ oz flour
10 ml/2 teaspoons lemon juice
300 ml/10 fl oz chicken stock
    (basic recipe)
salt and freshly ground black pepper
4 eggs
100 g/4 oz plain boiled or pilau
    rice (basic recipe)

Melt the butter in a heavy pan over
low heat and gently fry the onion for
about 10 minutes, until it has turned
golden brown. Then add the apple,
curry powder, the spices and flour,
and stir to blend evenly. Pour on
the lemon juice and then the stock
very gradually, stirring all the time
to prevent lumps from forming.
Bring the sauce to simmering point.
Season with salt and freshly ground
black pepper and simmer very
gently for 30 minutes, covered.
Meanwhile put the eggs into a saucepan
of cold water, bring to the boil,
then simmer for exactly 7 minutes.
Peel the shells from the cooked eggs,
cut them into quarters and place in a
warm serving dish.
Pour the curry sauce over the eggs.
Serve with pilau rice and mango chutney.

Braised Pork with Apples

 ①

Preparation and cooking time:
1 hour 20 minutes

450 g/1 lb lean belly pork strips
a little lard or dripping
salt and freshly ground black pepper
5 ml/1 teaspoon dried sage
1 large onion, sliced
1 large cooking apple, peeled, cored
    and chopped
30 ml/2 tablespoons water
350 g/12 oz potatoes
a little butter

Heat the oven to 375°F (Gas Mark 5,
190°C).
Trim off a little of the surplus fat
from the edge of the pork strips, then
fry them in lard or dripping to brown
on both sides.
Lay the pork strips on the bottom of
a casserole and season with salt and
freshly ground black pepper. Sprinkle
on the dried sage.
Fry the onion to a pale golden colour
then arrange over the pork together
with the chopped apple. Season with
a little more salt and pepper, and
pour on the water.
Peel and slice the potatoes thinly and
arrange them on top of the casserole
—overlapping like slates on a roof.
Season with more pepper and salt,
dot with a few flecks of butter and
bake, uncovered, for 1 hour. Serve
with a green vegetable.

*Opposite: Braised Pork with
Apples. Inset: Curried Eggs*

SUPPERS ON A TRAY

Here are recipes for when you want a quick delicious bite to eat before going out; for when you feel lazy and don't want to spend much time cooking; or for when you want to enjoy a cosy, casual meal. What could be nicer or more relaxed than supper on a tray! Make long, cold drinks and carry the tray into the garden on an evening when the weather is fine, or curl up by the fireside on a cold winter's night to watch television, listen to records, play chess or simply talk.

Spaghetti alla Carbonara

Preparation and cooking time:
15-20 minutes

225 g/8 oz spaghetti
salt
40 g/1½ oz butter
10 ml/2 teaspoons oil
half a medium-sized onion finely
    chopped
100 g/4 oz lean bacon, cut into strips
2 egg yolks
50 ml/2 fl oz single cream
120 ml/8 tablespoons finely grated
    Parmesan
freshly ground black pepper

Cook the spaghetti in a large saucepan of salted boiling water until 'al dente' —about 11 minutes.
Meanwhile heat the butter and oil together in a saucepan and sauté the onion in it until soft but not brown. Then add the bacon strips and cook for a further 5 minutes.
Blend the egg yolks together with the cream and 90 ml/6 tablespoons of grated Parmesan
When the spaghetti is cooked, drain in a colander and return it to a dry hot pan. Pour the bacon and onion mixture over the spaghetti, followed by the egg and cream. Toss thoroughly and season with salt and pepper.
Serve immediately with the remaining Parmesan cheese sprinkled over.

Chef's Salad

Preparation time:
10 minutes
This is basically a cold meat salad. It can be adapted for any cold meats that are available, and whatever salad vegetables are in season at the time.

100 g/4 oz cold roast beef
100 g/4 oz cooked ham
100 g/4 oz Swiss cheese
1 small lettuce heart
1 hardboiled egg, cut in half
2 tomatoes, quartered
2 celery stalks, finely chopped
1 small onion, finely chopped
4 sprigs of watercress

Cut the beef and ham into thin strips, also the cheese.
Divide the lettuce leaves between them on 2 plates. Arrange the strips of beef, ham and cheese on the lettuce leaves and place the hardboiled egg and tomato around them.
Sprinkle the chopped onion and celery all over and garnish with sprigs of watercress.
Serve with crusty fresh bread and a well flavoured vinaigrette dressing.

Salmon Loaf

Preparation time:
10 minutes plus 4 hours
This is a perfect dish for a summer evening, even if fresh salmon is beyond your budget. It should be served with a cucumber salad and some crusty fresh bread and butter.

200 g/7 oz canned salmon
50 g/2 oz butter, at room
    temperature
15 ml/1 tablespoon mayonnaise
1 small onion, grated
1 celery stalk, finely chopped
15 ml/1 tablespoon chopped parsley
a pinch of salt
a pinch of cayenne pepper
4 sprigs of watercress
1 hard-boiled egg

Turn the salmon out into a mixing bowl and mash to a pulp with a fork. Add the butter and mayonnaise and mix thoroughly until it becomes a smooth paste. Add the grated onion, celery, parsley, salt and cayenne pepper and mix thoroughly together.
Press the mixture into a small loaf tin or mould, cover lightly with aluminium foil and chill in the refrigerator for 4 hours.
To serve turn the salmon loaf out onto a serving dish and decorate with watercress and the hardboiled egg cut into slices.

Opposite: Spaghetti Alla Carbonara with a crisp, green salad

COOK AHEAD DISHES

Spiced Chicken

☆ ① ⊠ ⊠ ⊠

Preparation and cooking time:
1 hour plus 4 hours
This recipe is not quite a curry, but is
mildly spiced. Its distinctive taste is a
delicious way to flavour ordinary
supermarket chicken.

2 chicken breasts
1 garlic clove, crushed
salt and freshly ground black pepper
5 ml/1 teaspoon ground turmeric
5 ml/1 teaspoon ground ginger
5 ml/1 teaspoon curry powder
a little olive oil
25 g/1 oz butter
1 large onion, chopped
30 ml/2 tablespoons natural yogurt
30 ml/2 tablespoons single cream

Place the chicken breasts in a small
roasting tin or oven-proof dish.
Prick the flesh all over with a skewer
and rub in the crushed garlic. Season
with salt and pepper.
Mix the spices together, then sprinkle
a third of the mixture over the
chicken. Pour a little olive oil over
and using your hands rub the spices
well into the meat. Cover the dish with
aluminium foil and leave in a cool
place for 3-4 hours.
Heat the oven to 350°F (Gas Mark 4,
180°C).
Spread the butter on to the chicken,
re-cover the dish with foil and bake
in the oven for 30 minutes.
Meanwhile gently fry the onion in a
little olive oil for about 10 minutes
or until soft. Then stir in the
remainder of the spice mixture, the
yogurt and cream.
Remove the chicken from the oven,
pour the spiced onion and yogurt
mixture over it, re-cover and bake for
a further 30 minutes.
10 minutes before the end of cooking
time remove the foil and baste
the chicken with the sauce.
If you are cooking only a little ahead
of the meal time, the dish can simply
remain in the oven—at low heat—for

Opposite: Cannelloni

an extra hour or so without coming to
any harm.
To reheat next day, put the covered
chicken dish in the oven (pre-heated
to the temperature stated above) for
20-25 minutes.

Cannelloni

☆ ① ⊠ ⊠

Preparation and cooking time:
1 hour 20 minutes

pancake batter (basic recipe)
300 ml/10 fl oz cheese sauce
 (basic recipe)
freshly grated nutmeg
15 ml/1 tablespoon grated Parmesan
For the filling:
1 onion, finely chopped
1 garlic clove, crushed
30 ml/2 tablespoons oil
225 g/8 oz minced beef
1.25 ml/¼ teaspoon dried thyme
5 ml/1 teaspoon dried basil
10 ml/2 teaspoons tomato purée
225 g/8 oz canned tomatoes
salt and freshly ground black pepper

First make the filling: in a saucepan
gently fry the onions and garlic in
the oil for about 10 minutes, then
add the minced beef and cook to
brown it, carefully stirring all the
time to keep it separate.
Add the thyme, basil, tomato purée,
canned tomatoes and their liquid.
Stir thoroughly to amalgamate
everything, season with salt and
black pepper, and leave to cook over
very gentle heat for about 30 minutes
or until the meat is cooked.
Heat the oven to 425°F (Gas Mark 7,
220°C).
Meanwhile make the pancakes and
cheese sauce, and butter an oven-proof
dish. When the filling is ready place a
little on each pancake, roll up and
arrange in the buttered dish. Cover
the pancakes with the cheese sauce,
sprinkle over some freshly grated
nutmeg and the Parmesan. Bake for
20-30 minutes or until the top is golden.

Duck

☆ ① ① ① ⊠ ⊠ ⊠

Preparation and cooking time:
2¾ hours
One duck is usually too much for 2
people, so buy a good-sized bird
(2.75 kg/6 lb) and divide into 4
portions. 2 portions can be eaten
cold with fresh orange salad, the
others can be reheated and served
with cherry sauce (basic recipe).

1 x 2.75 kg/6 lb oven-ready duck
5 ml/1 teaspoon salt
2 medium-sized oranges
15 ml/1 tablespoon finely chopped mint
30 ml/1 tablespoon French dressing
4 sprigs of watercress

Heat the oven to 425°F (Gas Mark 7,
22°C).
Place the duck in a roasting tin and
prick the flesh all over with a
skewer—this allows surplus fat to
run out while cooking. Sprinkle the
bird with salt, but do *not* add any
fat at all.
Roast on the top shelf of the oven for
20 minutes. Then reduce the heat to
350°F (Gas Mark 4, 180°C) and cook
for a further 2¼ hours. During the
cooking drain off some of the fat
from the bottom of the roasting tin
2 or 3 times.
When cooked, remove the duck from
the roasting tin and cut it into
quarters with a very sharp pair of
scissors. Allow to cool, then wrap
each piece loosely in aluminium foil
to keep moist and store in a cool
place.
To prepare the salad, peel the oranges
and remove all the white pith. Slice
the flesh thinly with a sharp knife.
Sprinkle on the chopped mint and
vinaigrette. Unwrap 2 pieces of duck,
decorate with sprigs of watercress,
and serve with the salad.
To reheat the other 2 portions of
duck preheat the oven to 425°F (Gas
Mark 7, 220°C) and cook for 10-15
minutes till crisp. Serve with cherry
sauce (basic recipe), peas and new
potatoes.

WEIGHTWATCHERS' SPREAD

When you are calorie-counting, it is usually boredom and monotony of diet that leads to failure. We all know that eggs, meat and fish provide satisfying protein, but there is a limit to how much steak, omelette and steamed fish one can eat without craving for something more interesting. And it is even worse when you have to apologise for inflicting your tedious diet on another person. So here are 3 very low calorie dishes that will provide interest as well as nutrients—in fact, they are delicious even if you are not dieting.

Poached Trout with Herbs

 ① ① ⊠

Preparation and cooking time: *15 minutes*

2 large rainbow trout
salt
freshly ground black pepper
30 ml/2 tablespoons freshly chopped parsley
2 bay leaves
5 ml/1 teaspoon dried thyme
4 slice of lemon
15 ml/1 tablespoon wine vinegar

Wash and clean the trout, but do not remove the heads.
Place them in a large, deep frying pan. Season with salt and black pepper. Sprinkle on the chopped parsley, bay leaves and thyme. Also add the lemon slices. Pour on 15 ml/1 tablespoon of wine vinegar and enough cold water just to cover the fish.
Bring to simmering point and simmer for 6 minutes if the trout were fresh, or 10 minutes if they were frozen.

When cooked lift out the fish on a slice and drain on absorbent kitchen paper for a few minutes.
Serve on warmed plates with a mixed side salad.

Steak Tartare

 ① ① ① ⊠

Preparation time: *5 minutes*
Here's a delicious, nutritious and slimming dish that requires no cooking at all: both the egg and meat are raw. Use a really fresh egg and best quality steak very finely minced.

450 g/1 lb lean minced best fillet or rump steak
salt
freshly ground black pepper
5 ml/1 teaspoon olive oil
1 small onion, finely chopped
15 ml/1 tablespoon capers
5 ml/1 teaspoon Worcestershire sauce
15 ml/1 tablespoon finely chopped parsley
1 small egg

Season the steak with plenty of salt and freshly ground pepper. Add the oil, onion, capers and Worcestershire sauce and mix everything very thoroughly.
Separate the egg and mix the white into the meat.
Arrange the steak mixture in a mould

on a large plate and sprinkle with the freshly chopped parsley. Make a small well in the centre and place the egg yolk in it.
Mix the yolk into the steak at the dining table, and serve the tartare with a raw spinach salad.

Piperade Basque

 ①

Preparation and cooking time: *25 minutes*

1 medium-sized onion, chopped
a little olive oil
1 small green pepper, chopped
4 medium-sized tomatoes, skinned and chopped
salt
freshly ground black pepper
4 large eggs

Fry the onion in very little oil until it is soft—about 10 minutes. Then add the pepper to the pan and continue cooking for a further 6 minutes. Add the tomatoes, season with salt and pepper and heat through.
Pour a little oil into an omelette pan, just enough to moisten it all over the base and sides.
Beat 2 eggs lightly, season with pepper and salt and pour them into the very hot pan.
Put half the onion and pepper mixture into the centre of the eggs, then start to draw the edges towards the middle tipping the remaining egg liquid back to the sides of the pan. When all the liquid has been absorbed fold one edge over, then the other and slide the omelette on to a warmed plate. Keep warm.
Repeat with the other two eggs and remaining onion and pepper mixture.
Serve with a mixed salad.

Opposite top: Piperade Basque; centre: Steak Tartare; bottom: Poached Trout with Herbs

18

MEALS WITHOUT MEAT

Hazelnut and Tomato Rissoles

Preparation and cooking time:
35-40 minutes plus 1 hour
Serve these rissoles with a tomato or onion sauce, and accompanied by a green salad—and it will tempt even the most avid of steak fans.

15 ml/1 tablespoon olive oil
1 medium-sized onion, finely
   chopped
1 garlic clove crushed
450 g/1 lb tomatoes, skinned
10 ml/2 teaspoons tomato purée
2.5 ml/½ teaspoon dried basil
1.25 ml/¼ teaspoon dried thyme
a little grated lemon zest
225 g/8 oz mashed potato
175 g/6 oz hazelnuts, finely
   chopped
15 ml/1 tablespoon chopped parsley
salt
freshly ground black pepper
1 egg, beaten
stale white breadcrumbs

Heat the oil in a medium-sized saucepan and gently fry the onion and garlic until the onion is soft and golden. Chop the tomatoes and add them to the pan, together with the tomato purée, herbs and lemon zest. Cook until the mixture is reduced to a thick, jam-like consistency.
Combine the tomato mixture with the mashed potato. Stir in the chopped nuts and parsley. Mix to a fairly stiff but workable consistency. Season with salt and pepper.
Shape the mixture into flat round cakes. (If the mixture is too soft, chill it for 1 hour in the refrigerator first.) Dip the rissoles in beaten egg, and roll them evenly in breadcrumbs.
Heat a pan of deep oil to 375°F (190°C). Deep fry the rissoles for 1-2 minutes or until golden brown. Drain on kitchen paper and serve at once.

Opposite: Vegetable Curry

Cauliflower Cheese

Preparation and cooking time:
20-25 minutes

1 medium-sized cauliflower
salt
15 g/½ oz butter
15 ml/1 tablespoon oil
1 celery stalk, thinly sliced
1 medium-sized onion,
   chopped
30 ml/2 tablespoons flour
300 ml/10 fl oz milk
5 ml/1 teaspoon prepared French
   mustard
400 g/4 oz mature Cheddar cheese
freshly ground black pepper
3 tomatoes

Prepare the cauliflower by cutting off the base of the stem and most of the tough outer leaves. Hollow out the centre stalk, using a potato peeler. Cook the cauliflower for 8-10 minutes in a pan with 1.5 cm/½ in of boiling water. Keep the saucepan covered with a well-fitting lid.
Meanwhile prepare the sauce. Heat the butter and oil together in a saucepan and fry the sliced celery over moderate heat for 5 minutes. Add the chopped onion. Cook for a further 5 minutes, or until the vegetables are softened but not browned.
Add the flour, stir and cook for 1-2 minutes then gradually add the milk. Bring the sauce to the boil, stirring, then simmer for 2-3 minutes until it thickens.
Add the mustard and the cheese into the sauce, and season with salt and pepper.
Halve the tomatoes, season and dot with butter. Cook under a hot grill until just soft.
Drain the cauliflower and place in a warmed oven-proof dish. Pour the cheese sauce over and surround with tomato halves. Brown the cauliflower cheese for a few minutes under a hot grill before serving.

Vegetable Curry

Preparation and cooking time:
55 minutes

This is a moderately hot curry, depending of course on the brand of curry powder or paste you use.

100 g/4 oz carrots, sliced
salt
225 g/8 oz potatoes, diced
15 g/½ oz butter
15 ml/1 tablespoon olive oil
1 celery stalk, sliced
1 medium-sized onion, sliced
1 small cooking apple, peeled cored
   and diced
3 courgettes, sliced
15 ml/1 tablespoon flour
15 ml/1 tablespoon curry powder or
   paste
15 ml/1 tablespoon tomato purée
15 g/½ oz sultanas or
   raisins
the juice of half a lemon

Cook the carrots in a pan of boiling salted water for 5 minutes. Add the potatoes, bring back to the boil and simmer for a further 8 minutes. Drain the vegetables, reserving the liquid and keep warm.
Heat the butter and oil together in a medium-sized saucepan. Add the celery, onion, apple and courgettes and fry together gently for 5 minutes. Add the flour and curry powder or paste and fry for a further 5 minutes, stirring.
Measure a generous 300 ml/10 fl oz of the vegetable liquid, pour it on to the curry mixture and add the tomato purée and sultanas or raisins. Bring to the boil, stirring continuously Simmer uncovered for 15 minutes, stirring occasionally.
Add the carrots and potatoes. Cover and cook for a further 15 minutes. Taste and flavour with lemon juice, adding more seasoning if necessary.
Arrange a ring of hot cooked rice on a serving dish. Pile the curry into the centre.

CHEESE FOR TWO

Quite apart from its high nutritional value, cheese has the virtue of nearly always being available in everyone's kitchen. It is therefore ideal in emergencies.

Alpine Eggs

Preparation and cooking time:
20 minutes

40 g/1½ oz butter
175 g/6 oz Cheddar cheese, grated
4 large eggs
salt
freshly ground black pepper

Heat the oven to 375°F (Gas Mark 5, 190°C).
Generously butter a shallow fireproof baking dish and arrange half the grated cheese over the bottom.
Carefully break the eggs over the cheese, keeping the yolks whole. Season with salt and freshly ground black pepper. Cover the eggs completely with the rest of the grated cheese and dot with remaining butter.
Bake in the oven for about 10-15 minutes, until the top is golden-brown and bubbling and the yolks are just firm.

Cheese Scones

Preparation and cooking time:
25 minutes
Warm cheese scones, split and spread with lots of creamy butter are perfect for tea on a winter's day.

225 g/8 oz self-raising flour
a pinch of salt
a pinch of cayenne pepper
40 g/1½ oz butter
100 g/4 oz Cheddar cheese, finely grated
150 ml/5 fl oz milk

Heat the oven to 425°F (Gas Mark 7, 220°C).
Sift the flour and salt into a mixing-bowl, and add a pinch of cayenne pepper. Rub the butter into the flour till the mixture resembles fine bread-crumbs. Mix in the grated cheese. Add enough milk to the mixture to make an elastic dough.
Transfer on to a floured pastry board and roll out to 2 cm/¾ in thick. Cut into rounds with a 5 cm/2 in cutter. Brush the scones with milk and place on a greased baking tray.
Bake in the oven for 10-15 minutes until golden-brown.

Cheese, Egg and Mushroom Tart

Preparation and cooking time:
35-40 minutes

100 g/4 oz shortcrust pastry
100 g/4 oz mushrooms
50 g/2 oz butter
4 large eggs
25 g/1 oz flour
300 ml/10 fl oz milk
75 g/3 oz cheese, grated
salt
freshly ground black pepper
freshly ground nutmeg

Heat the oven to 375°F (Gas Mark 5, 190°C).
Line a 18 cm/7 in flan tin with the pastry. Prick the pastry base with a fork, then bake blind for 20 minutes.
Meanwhile, sauté the mushrooms in approximately one-quarter of the butter, and boil the eggs for 10 minutes.

Then make the sauce. Melt two-thirds of remaining butter in a small pan over gentle heat, stir in the flour, then add the milk a little at a time. When the mixture is smooth and thick, stir in two-thirds of the cheese and season well with salt, pepper and nutmeg. Cook the sauce over gentle heat for 5 minutes.
Remove the tart from the oven and increase the heat to 425°F (Gas Mark 7, 220°C).
Cool the cooked eggs under cold running water, then peel and slice them.
Lay the eggs and mushrooms on the bottom of the pastry case, and pour the sauce over them. Sprinkle the remaining cheese over the top. Cut the remaining butter into flecks and dot over the top.
Return the tart to the oven for 5-6 minutes or until the cheese has melted.
Serve with a fresh green salad.

Coeurs à la Crème

Preparation time:
10 minutes plus 8 hours

100 g/4 oz unsalted cream cheese
150 ml/5 fl oz sour cream
15 ml/1 tablespoon caster sugar
1 large egg white

In a mixing bowl, thoroughly combine the cream cheese, sour cream and sugar, then whisk the egg white till stiff and fold it carefully into the mixture.
Spoon the mixture into individual perforated dishes (or place it on a piece of cheesecloth in a sieve over a bowl) and leave in a cool place overnight to drain thoroughly.
Serve the crèmes topped with fresh raspberries or strawberries. A little fresh cream can be poured over if desired.

Top: Alpine Eggs; Cheese Scones.
Inset: Coeurs à la Crème

A VERY SPECIAL OCCASION

There are special occasions—such as a birthday or your wedding anniversary—when you want to splash out a bit, present a meal that is deliciously out of the ordinary and in keeping with your celebratory mood.

Here is a three-course meal that fills the bill perfectly. You want to look your best and relax together with a pre-dinner drink, so there's no last minute cooking, and two of the dishes are completely prepared well in advance.

Light the candles and enjoy your special evening.

Smoked Salmon and Trout Pâté

☆ ① ① ☒ ☒ ☒

Preparation time:
15 minutes plus 5 hours

This pâté can be made with a great variety of smoked fish (kipper, buckling or smoked eel, for instance) but it is best of all using a mixture of smoked salmon and trout, as here.

Take extra care when setting the table for a special occasion. Flowers, candles, pretty china and linen add a warm, intimate atmosphere.
Many other recipes can be used to good effect besides those given on this page. Shown opposite: Grilled Mackerel with Gooseberry Sauce, and Pears with Chocolate Sauce
Inset: Figs with Pernod

50 g/2 oz smoked salmon (end bits will do)
1 small smoked trout
50 g/2 oz butter
5 ml/1 teaspoon finely chopped onion
salt
freshly ground black pepper
a little grated nutmeg

Chop the smoked salmon into very small pieces. Skin the trout and remove the flesh from the bones. Pound the trout flesh and salmon to a pulp and gradually work in the butter until you have a smooth paste. Add the chopped onion and mix thoroughly. Season with salt and pepper to taste and add a little grated nutmeg.

Press the mixture into 2 individual ramekin dishes, cover and chill thoroughly for 3-5 hours.

Serve the pâté garnished with sprigs of watercress, offer lemon quarters to squeeze over the pâté and hot toast to eat with it.

Veal Cutlets baked with Cream and Mushrooms

☆ ① ① ① ☒ ☒

Preparation and cooking time:
1 hour 10 minutes
A fairly rich dish that needs only a few boiled new potatoes and a crisp green salad to go with it.

2 veal chops
25 g/1 oz butter
5 ml/1 teaspoon oil
2.5 ml/1 teaspoon dried thyme
salt
freshly ground black pepper

100 g/4 oz mushrooms, sliced
15 ml/1 tablespoon lemon juice
15 ml/1 tablespoon flour
50 ml/2 fl oz double cream

Heat the oven to 350°F (Gas Mark 4, 180°C).
Gently fry the veal chops in the butter and oil, enough to colour them slightly on both sides. Then place the chops on a large double sheet of aluminium foil in a roasting tin and sprinkle with thyme, salt and pepper. Fry the sliced mushrooms for 1-2 minutes, then add the lemon juice. Sprinkle on the flour and stir well.
Spread the mushroom mixture on to the chops. Pour the cream over and wrap the foil securely round the chops.
Bake in the oven for 1 hour.

Figs with Pernod

☆ ① ① ① ☒ ☒ ☒

Preparation time:
5 minutes, plus at least 3 hours
This is a luxury dessert which is very simple to prepare. The figs look particularly appetizing piled into a cut glass or silver bowl with extra cream in a matching jug.

300 g/11 oz canned figs in syrup
30 ml/2 tablespoons Pernod
50 ml/2 fl oz double cream
5 ml/1 teaspoon caster sugar

Tip the figs, together with their syrup, into a serving bowl. Stir in the Pernod, cover the bowl with aluminium foil and chill thoroughly in the refrigerator for at least 3 hours.
Whip the cream lightly with the sugar and serve the figs with the cream on top.

THE UNEXPECTED MEAL

Always be prepared for those embarrassing times when someone important arrives unexpectedly. Your store cupboard (if it's worthy of the name) should be able to cope with at least one complete meal. Below is a three course meal you will be able to rustle up quickly and with a minimum of fuss—and without anyone realizing it is straight off the store cupboard shelf.

French Onion Soup

Preparation and cooking time:
20 minutes
This is your first course. It's the cheat's version of Soupe à l'Onion Gratinée (if you're asked) and tastes very authentic. It is always advisable to keep a few canned soups in your cupboard to meet emergencies. And all soups can be jazzed up by the addition of cream, wine or sherry.

1 medium-sized onion, chopped
25 g/1 oz butter
300 ml/10 fl oz canned
    condensed onion soup
150 ml/5 fl oz dry white wine
salt and freshly ground black pepper
2 thick slices of French bread
40 g/1½ oz Emmenthal cheese,
    grated
10 ml/2 teaspoons grated Parmesan

Heat the oven to 450°F (Gas Mark 8, 230°C).
Fry the chopped onion in butter until it is soft.
Pour the canned soup and the white wine into a saucepan and heat to simmering point. Add the softened onion and some salt and pepper.
Toast the slices of bread on both sides.

Pour the soup into two oven-proof bowls, add the toasted bread, which should float on top, and sprinkle on the Emmenthal cheese. Place the bowls on a baking sheet in the oven and bake for about 10 minutes, or until the cheese has melted. *Sprinkle* with grated Parmesan and serve immediately.

Portuguese Fish Steaks

Preparation and cooking time:
30 minutes
Here is the main course—a complete store cupboard main course. If you're short of time, you can defrost the cod quickly by placing it (still in the wrapper) in a bowl of hot water.

4 frozen cod steaks, thawed
15 ml/1 tablespoon flour, seasoned
    with salt and ground pepper
olive oil
2.5 ml/½ teaspoon dried fennel
1 medium-sized onion, chopped
1 garlic clove, crushed
150 g/5 oz canned sweet red peppers,
    drained and chopped
175 g/6 oz canned tomatoes, drained

Heat the oven to 400°F (Gas Mark 6, 200°C).
Dry the cod steaks thoroughly with absorbent kitchen paper and cut them into large cubes. Toss them in the seasoned flour.
Heat some oil in a thick bottomed frying pan. Add the cubes of fish and cook until lightly browned.
Then transfer the fish to a lightly buttered casserole and sprinkle over the fennel.
Add the chopped onion and crushed garlic to the frying pan and fry them until pale golden, then add the chopped peppers and tomatoes. Heat them through and season generously with salt and pepper.
Pour the mixture over the fish and

bake, uncovered, for 15 minutes.
Serve wth tinned new potatoes heated through and then tossed in a little melted butter.

Lemon Soufflé Omelette Flambé

Preparation and cooking time:
10 minutes
The end to a perfect meal. Most people always have a lemon and a couple of eggs available to make this light and delicious dessert—but it is equally good made with orange.

3 large eggs
1 small lemon
15 ml/1 tablespoon caster sugar
25 g/1 oz butter
15 ml/1 tablespoon brandy

Separate the eggs. Add the juice and grated zest of lemon to the yolks, then add the sugar and whisk until slightly thickened.
Whisk the egg whites until they are stiff and form soft peaks.
Melt the butter in a thick-bottomed frying pan. Pre-heat the grill.
Carefully fold the egg yolk mixture into the whites then empty the mixture into the frying pan. Stir and fold with a metal spoon for a few seconds to prevent sticking.
Place the pan under the grill for a couple of minutes to allow the top of the omelette to brown lightly.
Warm a tablespoon and quickly pour the brandy into it. Set light to the spirit and pour the flaming brandy over the soufflé omelette while you are carrying it to the table.

Opposite: French Onion Soup.
Inset: Lemon Soufflé Omelette Flambé

SUNDAY BRUNCH DANISH STYLE

Cooking a full scale Sunday lunch for two every week can seem extravagant and time consuming. Brunch—half breakfast and half lunch—is a much more versatile meal. But it is important to avoid making it a half-hearted substitute for a proper meal.

Smorrebrod, one of the mouth watering inventions of the Danes, is a colourful and filling answer. Basically Smorrebrod consists of open sandwiches, generously and imaginatively topped with a wide variety of foods. The bread should always be rye (of which there are

many types ranging from dark to light) spread thickly with butter. Here is a selection of traditional Danish toppings, which perhaps will inspire you to start inventing some of your own. If necessary use cocktail sticks to secure them.

Salad Shrimp

2 slices rye bread, buttered
2 lettuce leaves
30 ml/2 tablespoons mayonnaise
100 g/4 oz cooked and peeled shrimps
2 twists of lemon
2 sprigs of parsley
a little paprika

Place a lettuce leaf flat on each piece of bread. Place a line of shrimps diagonally across the centre of each slice. Pipe mayonnaise either side of the shrimps and then fill the corners with additional shrimps. Place a twist of lemon in the centre and sprigs of watercress either side. Sprinkle with a little paprika.

The Tivoli

2 slices buttered rye bread
2 lettuce leaves
6 slices of hard boiled egg
8 slices of tomato
25 g/1 oz smoked cod's roe
15 ml/1 tablespoon mayonnaise

Place a lettuce leaf on each piece of bread. Arrange the egg slices along one edge and the slices of tomato along the other. Pipe the cod's roe in a row of dots down the centre, and top with piped mayonnaise.

Hans Anderson

2 slices buttered rye bread
2 slices liver pâté
2 small pieces lettuce leaf
4 raw button mushrooms, sliced
2 slices of tomato
2 gherkins
2 bacon slices, crisply fried and drained

Place the slices of pâté on the buttered bread, then in one corner of each piece of bread lay the sliced mushrooms. In the opposite corner lay a tomato slice and a gherkin cut into a fan shape. Arrange the bacon slices diagonally, across the top.

The Mariner

2 slices buttered rye bread
6 strips rollmop herring
6 slices of tomato
6 onion rings
2 sprigs parsley

Arrange 3 herring fillets side by side, diagonally on each piece of bread, and tuck a tomato slice in between each herring. Place the onion rings over the top and garnish with a sprig of parsley.

Use your artistic talents to make Danish open sandwiches look attractive and delicious!

Danish Delight

2 slices buttered rye bread
4 small slices cold cooked pork
2 small lettuce leaves
15 ml/1 tablespoon pickled red cabbage
2 slices of orange (with peel)
2 prunes

Place 2 slices of pork overlapping on each piece of bread. Place a piece of lettuce in one corner and fill it with red cabbage. Place an orange twist in the other corner with a prune.

The Copenhagen

2 slices buttered rye bread
6 slices pork luncheon meat
15 ml/1 tablespoon creamed horseradish
2 slices of orange (with peel)
4 prunes, soaked and stoned
2 sprigs watercress

Fold the slices of luncheon meat into rolls and place 3 side by side on each piece of bread. Spoon the creamed horseradish into the centre of each roll and place a twisted orange slice on top. Arrange a prune on either side, and add a sprig of watercress to one side.

SUNDAY BRUNCH AMERICAN STYLE

Few people are as relaxed about their eating as the Americans, and since Sunday should be a day of relaxation, why not follow their example now and again? The famous 'dips and dunks' for instance are one of the easiest things to eat. Once you've made your dip, all you'll need are lots of dippy foods like potato crisps strips of raw vegetables such as salted biscuits cocktail sausages and, perhaps nicest of all, long carrots.

Guacamole

half a ripe avocado pear
10 ml/2 teaspoons lemon juice
1 garlic clove, crushed
a pinch of chilli powder
a dash of tabasco
5 ml/1 teaspoon onion, finely minced
15 ml/1 tablespoon mayonnaise
salt
freshly ground black pepper

Scoop out all the flesh from the avocado and mash it to a pulp with a fork. Add the lemon juice, garlic, chilli powder, tabasco and raw onion. Stir in the mayonnaise and season with salt and pepper. Blend everything together thoroughly. Cover and chill.
(*Note:* it is best not to make this dip more than 3-4 hours in advance because it tends to discolour if left too long.)

Garlic Cheese Dip

1 garlic clove, crushed
50 g/2 oz cream cheese
5 ml/1 teaspoon minced raw onion

10 ml/2 teaspoons finely chopped
   chives
salt
freshly ground black pepper
Blend everything together thoroughly and chill.

The Californian Hamburger

Real American hamburgers, properly made, are every bit as good as an ordinary steak—if not better. If the weather is good, the very best way to cook them is outside over a charcoal grill, but they're none the worse for being cooked under a hot electric or gas grill.

225 g/8 oz minced sirloin (80%
   lean, 20% fat)
salt
freshly ground black pepper
a little oil
2 slices raw onion
10 ml/2 teaspoons mayonnaise
10 ml/2 teaspoons relish
2 slices of tomato
4 slices pickled dill cucumber
2 large sesame seed buns

First switch the grill to the highest setting—fierce heat is important

for initial cooking.
Season the beef with plenty of salt and freshly ground pepper. Divide into 2 portions and shape each one into a round patty about 4 cm/1½ in thick.
Place patties on the grill pan and brush with a little oil on both sides. Grill for about 1 minute each side, then lower the heat and cook for about 5 minutes more on each side for medium cooked—or more or less according to taste.
Toast the sesame buns on the inside. Place the onion rings and a little mayonnaise on each bun. Then put a hamburger on top, followed by the slice of tomato, the dill cucumber and finally the relish. Top with the other half of the bun and serve.

Hot Chocolate Fudge Sundae

2 portions of vanilla ice-cream
100 g/4 oz plain chocolate
15 ml/1 tablespoon water
15 g/½ oz butter
15 ml/1 tablespoon toasted almonds
wafer biscuits

Heat the oven to 350°F (Gas Mark 4, 180°C).
Break up the chocolate into a heat-proof dish, add the water and place on the lowest shelf of the oven for 12 minutes to melt.
Remove from the oven and beat till smooth, adding the butter. Scoop the ice-cream into sundae glasses, pour over the hot chocolate and sprinkle with toasted almonds.
Serve with wafer biscuits.

A mixture of textures and tastes can be served at a friendly American-style brunch. Shown opposite: Guacomole and Garlic Cheese Dip, The Californian Hamburger and Hot Chocolate Fudge Sundae

COLD FOOD FOR PICNICS

Below: A pretty country spot on a warm summer's day: ideal for a relaxing picnic. Left: Banana and Walnut Cake

When planning a picnic it is very important to choose the right foods and the right containers in which to transport them. Consider how the meal is to be eaten and carried and bear in mind the season. Wide-necked vacuum flasks now enable you to take ice-creams and sorbets but do remember to put hot foods into a warmed flask and cold food into chilled flasks — this will give both several hours more life.

Picnic Pâté

Preparation and cooking time:
2 hours plus 5 hours
To be at its best the pâté should be made 2 days in advance.

225 g/8 oz pork liver
225 g/8 oz fat belly of pork, rind removed
1 small onion, finely chopped
1 garlic clove, crushed
45 ml/3 tablespoons brandy
45 ml/3 tablespoons Madeira
2.5 ml/½ teaspoon salt
1.25 ml/¼ teaspoon ground allspice
freshly ground black pepper
225 g/8 oz thinly sliced streaky bacon
100 g/4 oz chicken livers, cleaned
1 bay leaf
5 ml/1 teaspoon powdered gelatine

Heat the oven to 325°F (Gas Mark 3, 170°C).
Coarsely mince the liver and belly of pork into a bowl. Add the chopped onion, crushed garlic, brandy, Madeira, salt, allspice and pepper to taste. Blend thoroughly with a wooden spoon—the mixture will be rather moist at this stage.
Separate the chicken livers into lobes and stir into the pâté mixture.
Line the base and sides of a 900 ml/ 1½ pint loaf tin with the bacon.
Pour the mixture into the lined tin. Cover the top with more bacon slices and lay the bayleaf in the centre. Cover the tin well with a double layer of aluminium foil. Place in a roasting tin and pour in boiling water to come a third of the way up the side of the tin.
Bake in the oven for 1½ hours or until the juices run clear when a skewer is pushed through the centre of the pâté.
Remove the aluminium foil from the

cooked pâté and place a plate and a heavy weight on top of the pâté. Leave for 15 minutes then pour off the surplus juices into a bowl.
Sprinkle the gelatine onto the juices and leave to stand for a few minutes. Then place the bowl in a pan of hot water and stir until the gelatine is completely dissolved. Pour over the pâté and weight it again for 4-5 hours until cold.

Picnic Pie

Preparation and cooking time:
1¼ hours
If you have a 18 cm/7 inch plate on which to bake this pie, so much the better. Line and cover the pie plate in the normal way, and take the pie on your picnic still on the plate, securely wrapped in foil. Alternatively, bake the pie straight on the baking tray as in the recipe then transport it wrapped in foil and tightly sealed inside a plastic bag.

225 g/8 oz back of rib of veal
225 g/8 oz chump end of pork
2 streaky bacon slices, diced
1 small potato, diced
1 small garlic clove, crushed
a pinch of dried thyme
1.25 ml/¼ teaspoon ground allspice
2.5 ml/½ teaspoon salt
freshly ground black pepper
15 ml/ 1 tablespoon stock
30 ml/2 tablespoons chopped parsley
175 g/6 oz. shortcrust pastry
1 egg, beaten

Heat the oven to 400°F (Gas Mark 6, 200°C).
Trim excess fat from the meat and cut the meat into small pieces. Place it in a large bowl and mix in all the remaining ingredients with the exception of the pastry and beaten egg.
Cut off one-third of the pastry and set the rest aside. On a lightly floured surface, roll out the smaller piece of pastry. Using a saucepan lid as a guide, cut out a circle 20 cm/8 in diameter. Place on a baking sheet.
Knead the pastry trimmings lightly into the remaining pastry. Roll out and cut a 23 cm/9 inch circle, again using a suitably sized plate or lid as a guide.
Pile the prepared meat mixture onto the smaller pastry round on the baking

sheet, leaving a clear 1.5 cm/½ inch around the edge. Brush the border with beaten egg. Lift the larger pastry round, over a rolling pin, and cover the meat. Pinch the pastry edges together firmly to seal, then decorate.
Knead and roll out the pastry trimmings and cut into leaf-shapes to decorate the top of the pie. Make a steam hole in the centre and glaze the pie all over with beaten egg.
Bake the pie for 10 minutes then reduce heat to 350°F (Gas Mark 4, 180°C) and bake for a further 65 minutes, or until the pie is golden-brown. Cover the pie with foil if it seems to be browning too much before the end of the cooking time.

Banana and Walnut Cake

Preparation and cooking time:
1 hour 10 minutes
This cake is delicious when served thickly sliced and spread with butter. It also keeps particularly well stored in an airtight tin.

40 g/1½ oz butter
40 g/1½ oz lard
100 g/4 oz caster sugar
1 egg, beaten
the grated zest of 1 lemon
the grated zest of 1 orange
225 g/8 oz flour
10 ml/2 teaspoons baking powder
4 medium-sized bananas
50 g/2 oz shelled walnuts, chopped coarsely

Heat the oven to 350°F (Gas Mark 4, 180°C).
Cream the fats with the sugar and beat until light and fluffy. Beat in the egg and grated zest of orange and lemon. Sift the flour and baking powder together and add to the creamed mixture.
Place the bananas in a small bowl and mash with a fork. Then add to the cake mixture together with the chopped walnuts.
Turn the cake mixture into a buttered 23 x 12.5 cm/9 x 5 inch loaf tin and level off the top. Bake for 50 minutes or until a skewer inserted through the thickest part of the cake comes out clean. Turn out onto a cake rack and allow to cool.

APPETIZERS

On the next two pages you will
find a selection of recipes to
get your meal off to a delicious
start—mousses, salads and a warm
soup for a cold day. The main
ingredients are fish, cheese and a
variety of vegetables.

Smoked Salmon Mousse

Preparation time:
15 minutes, plus 1 hour
This is a lovely way to make use of those end bits of smoked salmon sold quite cheaply at many delicatessen counters. For a really festive touch you could garnish the mousse most attractively with bands of tiny petit pois and red salmon caviar.

100 g/4 oz smoked salmon pieces
60 ml/4 tablespoons single cream
5 ml/1 teaspoon lemon juice
salt
freshly ground black pepper
freshly ground nutmeg
45 ml/3 tablespoons liquid aspic
1 egg white
150 ml/5 fl oz double cream

Chop the smoked salmon coarsely. Put it into a blender, or through a food mill, together with the single cream, lemon juice, a little salt, freshly ground black pepper and nutmeg. Blend it to a smooth purée then beat in 45 ml/3 tablespoons of liquid aspic.
Whisk the double cream until it is soft but firm, then fold it into the salmon mixture. Whisk the egg white until stiff but not dry and add it to the mixture. Taste and season again if necessary.
Pour the mousse into a small deep serving dish or individual ramekins and chill until set.
Serve with brown bread and butter or slices of toast.

Avocado Mousse

Preparation time:
25 minutes plus 3 hours
This mousse looks as good as it tastes when turned out of its mould and served on a bed of lettuce leaves. Decorate it with paper-thin slices of cucumber, tomato wedges and black olives.

Previous page top: Tuna Stuffed Lemons; left: Greek Island Salad; right: Courgettes à la Greque; bottom: Avocado and Seafood Salad

half a chicken stock cube
1 ripe avocado pear
the juice of 1 lemon
2.5 ml/½ teaspoon finely chopped chives
2.5 ml/½ teaspoon dried tarragon
2.5 ml/½ teaspoon onion juice
a dash of tabasco
10 g/¼ oz powdered gelatine
30 ml/2 tablespoons water
150 ml/5 fl oz double cream
salt
freshly ground black pepper

Dissolve the stock cube in 150 ml/5 fl oz of boiling water. Peel, stone and dice the avocado roughly. Put the diced avocado into an electric blender together with the stock, lemon juice, herbs, onion juice and tabasco, and blend until smooth, or pass the mixture through a nylon sieve. Pour into a bowl.
Sprinkle the gelatine over the water in a cup and leave for 5 minutes. When softened, place the cup in a bowl of hot water and stir until the gelatine is completely dissolved and the liquid is quite clear. When it is cool beat the dissolved gelatine into the avocado mixture.
Whip the cream lightly then fold it into the avocado mixture. Add salt and pepper to taste—the mixture should be highly seasoned.
When the mousse is cold but not set, pour into individual ramekins or one larger mould. Chill until set in the refrigerator.
To turn out the mould, dip into very hot water for a few seconds and invert onto a plate. Serve very cold.

Courgettes à la Grecque

Preparation and cooking time:
40 minutes plus 1 hour
Always choose small, even-sized courgettes. Never buy those which look as though they have ambitions to become marrows. Small courgettes will taste infinitely nicer and look far more attractive when served. In this recipe, the courgettes are cooked and simply garnished with chopped fresh parsley.

45 ml/3 tablespoons olive oil
1 medium-sized onion, finely chopped

1 garlic clove, crushed
60 ml/4 tablespoons dry white wine
60 ml/4 tablespoons water
a bouquet garni
6 coriander seeds
6 black peppercorns
1 small lemon
salt
350 g/12 oz small courgettes
30 ml/ 2 tablespoons chopped parsley

Heat 30 ml/2 tablespoons oil in a heavy pan or casserole; add the finely chopped onion and the garlic, and sauté until transparent. Add the wine and water, the bouquet garni, coriander seeds, black peppercorns, lemon juice and salt to taste. Bring to the boil and simmer for 5 minutes.
Trim the ends of the courgettes carefully and wipe the skins clean with a damp cloth. (Do not peel.) Quarter them and cut into 5 cm/2 inch segments. Add to the simmering sauce and cook over low heat for 20-25 minutes or until tender but still firm.
Transfer the courgettes to a deep serving dish, discard the bouquet garni and pour on the cooking juices. Then allow to cool and chill until ready to serve.
Just before serving, moisten with the remaining olive oil, sprinkle with finely chopped parsley and a little additional lemon juice to taste.

Chilled Seafood Appetizer

Preparation and cooking time:
1¼ hours plus 1 hour
Try this salad mixed with a French dressing, as in the recipe below, or alternatively coated with a well-flavoured mayonnaise.

75 g/3 oz long grain rice
1.2 L/2 pints mussels
15 cm/5 fl oz dry white wine
60 ml/4 tablespoons water
1 small onion, finely chopped
50 g/2 oz cooked, peeled shrimps
2 tomatoes, peeled
15 ml/1 tablespoon chopped parsley
15 ml/1 tablespoon grated onion
30 ml/2 tablespoons wine vinegar
60-75 ml/4-5 tablespoons olive oil
salt and freshly ground black pepper

Boil the rice in plenty of salted water, until the grains are tender but still firm. Drain thoroughly and set aside to cool.

Meanwhile scrub the mussels well, removing the 'beards' and discarding any shells that do not close. Place the mussels in a pan with the wine, water and finely chopped onion. Cover tightly with a lid and cook over high heat, shaking the pan frequently, until the mussels have all opened—about 5-7 minutes.

Remove the mussels from the pan, shaking back any liquid trapped in the shells. Strain the liquid through cheesecloth or a fine sieve lined with kitchen paper. Rinse out the pan and return the liquid to it. Add the shrimps and cook for 10 minutes.

Meanwhile remove the mussels from their shells, and discard any which have not opened.

Drain the shrimps and combine with the rice and mussels. Slice the tomatoes and add to the mixture, together with the chopped parsley.

Make a French dressing by combining the grated onion, vinegar and oil with a little salt and pepper. Combine all the ingredients thoroughly together with a fork. Pour over the salad and toss lightly. Chill before serving.

Avocado and Seafood Salad

Preparation time:
15 minutes

2 anchovy fillets
50 g/2 oz cooked, peeled prawns or shrimps
30 ml/2 tablespoons vinaigrette or thick mayonnaise
a little grated lemon zest
salt
freshly ground black pepper
1 ripe avocado pear
a squeeze of lemon juice

Remove all the oil from the anchovies by draining them on kitchen paper. Using a pair of scissors, snip the fillets into small pieces. Place them in a mixing bowl. Add the prawns or shrimps (reserving a few for garnish), mayonnaise or vinaigrette, and lemon zest. Stir to mix and season well.

Cut the avocado in half, remove the stone and peel the skin from the flesh. Cut the flesh, sprinkle on the lemon juice then add to the other ingredients in the bowl and mix lightly together.

Transfer the salad to a small serving dish and garnish with a whole prawn or shrimp and a twist of lemon.

Greek Island Salad

Preparation time:
10 minutes

This Greek salad is traditionally made with Fetta cheese. White Stilton is fairly similar, more widely available and perfectly adequate for this recipe.

75 g/3 oz Fetta cheese
3 large tomatoes, thinly sliced
1 onion, sliced in thin rings
6-8 black olives
1 medium-sized gherkin, sliced
5 ml/1 teaspoon finely crushed coriander seeds
1 garlic clove, crushed
2.5 ml/½ teaspoon oregano
30 ml/2 tablespoons olive oil
salt
freshly ground black pepper

Cut the cheese into fairly thin strips, 4 cm/1½ inches in length. Place the cheese in a salad bowl, add the tomatoes, onions, olives and gherkins and mix together.

In a small bowl combine the crushed coriander, crushed garlic and oregano with the olive oil, and pour over the salad. Season with salt and freshly ground black pepper and serve with hot fresh bread.

Leek and Potato Soup

Preparation and cooking time:
50 minutes

It seems a pity to make this delicious soup for just 2 portions and it's not so economical. So here we give quantities which will make enough for 2 people for 2 days as a first course, or enough for one complete meal for 2 people with fruit and cheese to follow.

4 large leeks, thoroughly cleaned
2 medium-sized potatoes, diced
1 medium-sized onion, diced
900 ml/1½ pints hot chicken stock
300 ml/10 fl oz milk
50 g/2 oz butter
10 ml/2 teaspoons dried chives
salt and freshly ground black pepper

Cut off the tops of the leeks, leaving the white part and 2.5 ml/1 inch green. Slice off the root end, split lengthways and slice finely.

Gently melt the butter in a saucepan, tip in the leeks, potatoes and onions and stir to coat evenly with the butter.

Keeping the heat fairly low, place the lid on the saucepan and sweat the vegetables for 10 minutes.

Then pour in the stock and the milk, stir again and season. Replace the lid and leave to simmer very gently for 20-25 minutes or until the vegetables are soft—watch carefully that it does not boil over.

Purée the soup in a blender or press it through a fine sieve. Taste to check seasoning, add the chives, re-heat and serve.

Tuna Stuffed Lemons

Preparation time:
15 minutes plus 30 minutes

2 large lemons
200 g/7 oz canned tuna fish, drained
50 g/2 oz butter
a pinch of dried thyme
5 ml/1 teaspoon Dijon mustard
2.5 ml/½ teaspoon paprika
salt and freshly ground black pepper
1 egg white
2 bay leaves

First slice the tops off the lemons and set them aside. Slice a little off the other end so the lemons will stand upright. Scoop out all the pulp and place in a sieve resting over a bowl. Press the juice through.

In another bowl mash the drained tuna with the butter, then add the mustard and seasonings. Stir in the lemon juice and finally whip the egg white until stiff and fold it into the mixture.

Taste to check the seasonings, fill the lemons with the mixture, replace caps and decorate each with a bay leaf. *Chill* for 30 minutes before serving.

A JOINT OF BEEF FOR THREE MEALS

1. Roast Beef with Roast Potatoes

Preparation and cooking time:
about 2¼ hours
Always allow meat plenty of time to come up to room temperature again if it has been stored in your refrigerator or the butcher's. It is a good idea to rub seasonings into the meat as soon as it comes out of the refrigerator, then leave it at room temperature for 2-3 hours, so that it can lose its chill and absorb the flavours at the same time.

1.5 kg/3½ lb topside of beef
salt
freshly ground black pepper
50 g/2 oz dripping or
**   butter**
750 g/1½ lb potatoes

Heat the oven to 425°F (Gas Mark 7, 220°C).
Wipe the joint dry and season with salt and pepper.
Heat the dripping or butter in a roasting tin and brown the joint well all over, over high heat. Set aside.
Peel the potatoes and cut into even-sized pieces. Drain thoroughly on kitchen paper, then turn the potatoes into the hot fat. Season well with salt and freshly ground black pepper. Stand a rack over the potatoes and place the joint on it.
Roast for 15 minutes then reduce the heat to 325°F (Gas Mark 3, 170°C). Calculate the roasting time at 15 minutes per pound for rare meat, 25 minutes for medium and 35 minutes for well done, and roast according to taste. Baste once or twice during the roasting, so that the potatoes absorb some of the juices.
When the meat is cooked to your liking remove the roasting tin from the oven and transfer the joint to a heated serving dish. Keep warm. Turn the oven up again to 425°F (Gas Mark 7, 220°C) and return the tin of potatoes to the oven to crisp. If you are baking a Yorkshire pudding, put it in at this point, near the top of the oven.)

2. Minced Beef Curry

Preparation and cooking time:
40 minutes
Curried food makes a pleasant change —and it's easy, convenient and economical. As with most types of stews and casseroles, a curry actually improves in flavour if kept overnight.

25 g/1 oz butter
1 medium-sized onion, finely
**   chopped**
1 apple, peeled, cored and chopped
30 ml/2 tablespoons curry powder, or
**   to taste**
15 ml/1 tablespoon flour
450 g/1 lb cooked beef, coarsely minced
300 ml/10 fl oz beef stock (or
**   thin gravy)**
15 ml/1 tablespoon mango chutney
25 g/1 oz sultanas
**   or raisins**
15 ml/1 tablespoon lemon juice
100 g/4 oz long-grain rice
salt
100 g/4 oz frozen peas
30 ml/2 tablespoons sour cream
**   (optional)**

Heat half of the butter in a medium-sized saucepan. Sauté the chopped onion and apple gently for 5 minutes. Stir in the curry powder and cook for a further 2 minutes. Add the flour, cooked minced beef, stock, mango chutney, sultanas or raisins and lemon juice. Bring to the boil, then simmer uncovered for 30 minutes, stirring occasionally to prevent the curry burning on the base of the pan.
About 15 minutes before the end of the cooking time, boil the rice in salted water, adding the frozen peas when the rice is half-cooked. Drain the rice and peas well. Toss with the remaining butter and arrange in a ring around the edge of a warmed serving dish.
Stir the sour cream (if used) into the curry. Taste and season if necessary, then pour the curry into the centre of the rice ring. Serve immediately.

3. Cottage Pie

Preparation and cooking time:
35-40 minutes
The recipe given below calls for packet mashed potato, but you can use 1 kg/ 2 lb of potatoes peeled, boiled and mashed with butter and cream, if you prefer.

1 Spanish onion, finely
**   chopped**
30 ml/2 tablespoons olive oil
450 g/1 lb cooked roast beef, coarsely
**   minced**
300 ml/10 fl oz beef gravy
10 ml/2 teaspoons Worcestershire
**   sauce**
30 ml/2 tablespoons finely chopped
**   parsley**
2.5 ml/½ teaspoon mixed herbs
salt and freshly ground black pepper
1 packet instant mashed potato
**   (2-3 servings)**

Heat the oven to 400°F (Gas Mark 6, 200°C).
Sauté the finely chopped onion in olive oil until soft and golden. Stir in the minced beef, gravy, Worcestershire sauce, chopped parsley and mixed herbs. Taste and season with salt and pepper. Remove the pan from the heat and turn in a deep oven-proof dish.
Make up the instant mashed potato according to instructions on the packet. Spread the mashed potato mixture over the heat in the baking dish.
Bake for 20-25 minutes or until the potato is tinged golden brown.

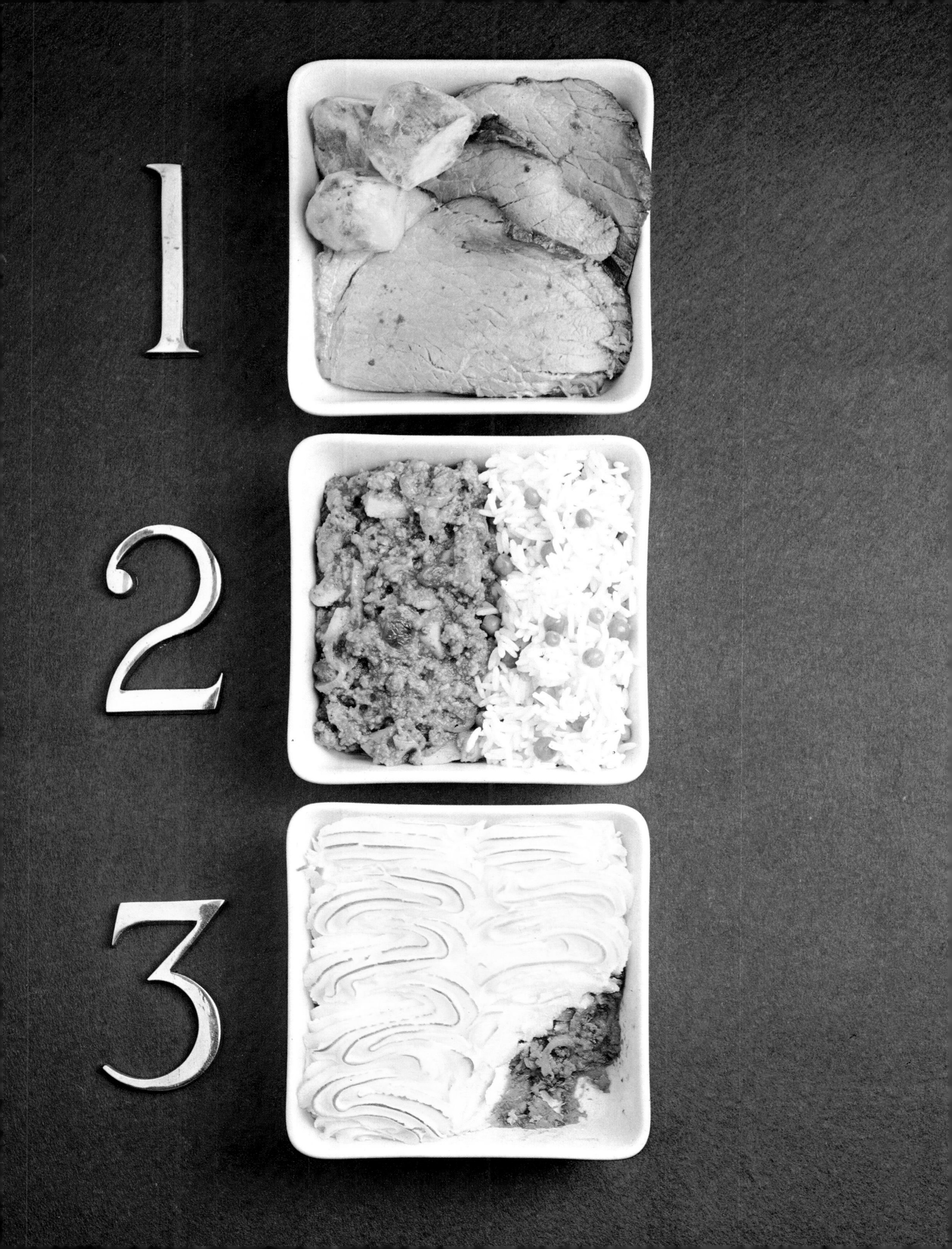
1
2
3

A JOINT OF LAMB FOR THREE MEALS

1. Roast Lamb with New Potatoes

☆ ① ① ☒ ☒

Preparation and cooking time:
about 2¼ hours
Before roasting, make sure you cut away all surplus fat from the surface of the joint to give an even layer of fat approximately 1 cm/¼ inch thick all round the meat.

1 x 2 kg/4½ lb leg of lamb
2 garlic cloves
65 g/2½ oz butter, at
**   room temperature**
5 ml/1 teaspoon dried rosemary
the juice of 1 lemon
salt
freshly ground black pepper
300 ml/10 fl oz beef stock
15 ml/1 tablespoon flour

Heat the oven to 400°F (Gas Mark 6, 200°C).
Wipe the joint clean with a damp cloth. Cut the garlic cloves into about 20 thin slivers. Make enough slits all over the meat to insert the garlic slivers. Mix 50 g/2 oz of softened butter with the rosemary, lemon juice, salt and pepper, and spread the butter mixture all over the meat.
Place the meat in a roasting pan and roast according to taste, allowing 23 minutes per 0.5 kg/1 lb for very pink, 27 minutes for pink and 30 minutes for well done lamb.
When the meat is cooked to your liking, transfer it to a heated serving dish and keep warm until ready to be carved.
Prepare the gravy by stirring the stock into the roasting pan and scraping the base and sides of the pan as you bring the stock to the boil. Make a paste of the remaining butter and flour, and add in small quantities to the hot stock, stirring constantly. Bring back to the boil and simmer for 2-3 minutes and pour into a heated sauceboat.

2. Deep-fried Lamb Croquettes

☆ ☆ ① ☒ ☒ ☒

Preparation and cooking time:
30 minutes plus 8 hours
This dish is best if the cooked meat mixture is set on a plate, covered and left overnight in the refrigerator. Coat with egg, roll in breadcrumbs and cook the croquettes next day.

25 g/1 oz butter
1 small onion, finely chopped
30 ml/2 tablespoons flour
300 ml/10 fl oz strong stock
350 g/12 oz cooked lamb, minced
30 ml/2 tablespoons chopped parsley
5 ml/1 teaspoon Worcestershire sauce
salt
freshly ground black pepper
1 egg
15 ml/1 tablespoon milk
fresh white breadcrumbs

Heat the butter in a medium-sized saucepan and sauté the chopped onion till soft and golden. Then stir in the flour and cook for 1-2 minutes. Gradually add the stock, stirring all the time. Bring to the boil and cook for 2-3 minutes. Stir in the meat, chopped parsley and Worcestershire sauce. Season with salt and freshly ground black pepper, if necessary.
Remove the pan from the heat. Spread the meat mixture onto a plate. Cover and leave to get cold, preferably overnight in a refrigerator.
When cold and set, divide the meat mixture into 8 equal portions. Roll into neat sausage shapes. In a shallow dish, beat the egg together with the milk. Coat each croquette with egg, then breadcrumbs—twice.
Heat a pan of deep oil to 375°F (190°C).
Deep-fry the croquettes for 2-3 minutes or until golden brown. Drain on kitchen paper and serve immediately accompanied by Courgettes with tomatoes (see Exciting Vegetables).

3. Turkish Lamb Pilaff

☆ ① ☒

Preparation and cooking time:
30 minutes
This dish is nicest served with sour cream or yogurt. Of course the basic ingredients can be added to or changed to accommodate the leftovers you happen to have available at the time.

60 ml/4 tablespoons oil
175 g/6 oz long grain rice
1.2 L/2 pints stock
25 g/1 oz butter
25 g/1 oz blanched
**   almonds**
1 onion, chopped
350 g/12 oz cooked lamb, cut into
**   strips**
25 g/1 oz raisins, plumped in
**   boiling water**
10 ml/2 teaspoons ground cinnamon
**   (optional)**
salt
freshly ground black pepper

In a heavy pan heat half of the oil. Add the rice and cook until it becomes transparent. Pour in the boiling stock and boil over high heat for about 12 minutes. Do not allow the rice to overcook.
Meanwhile, heat the remaining oil and butter in a pan and sauté the almonds in the hot fat until golden. Remove the nuts from the pan using a perforated spoon, and set aside.
Gently fry the chopped onion in the fat left in the pan. When it is soft and transparent add the meat and sauté until lightly browned and well heated through.
When the rice is just cooked, strain and add to the meat pan. Stir in the almonds and raisins and mix lightly with a fork. Season to taste with salt and pepper, cinnamon if used. Allow the pilaff to heat through gently, then serve immediately.

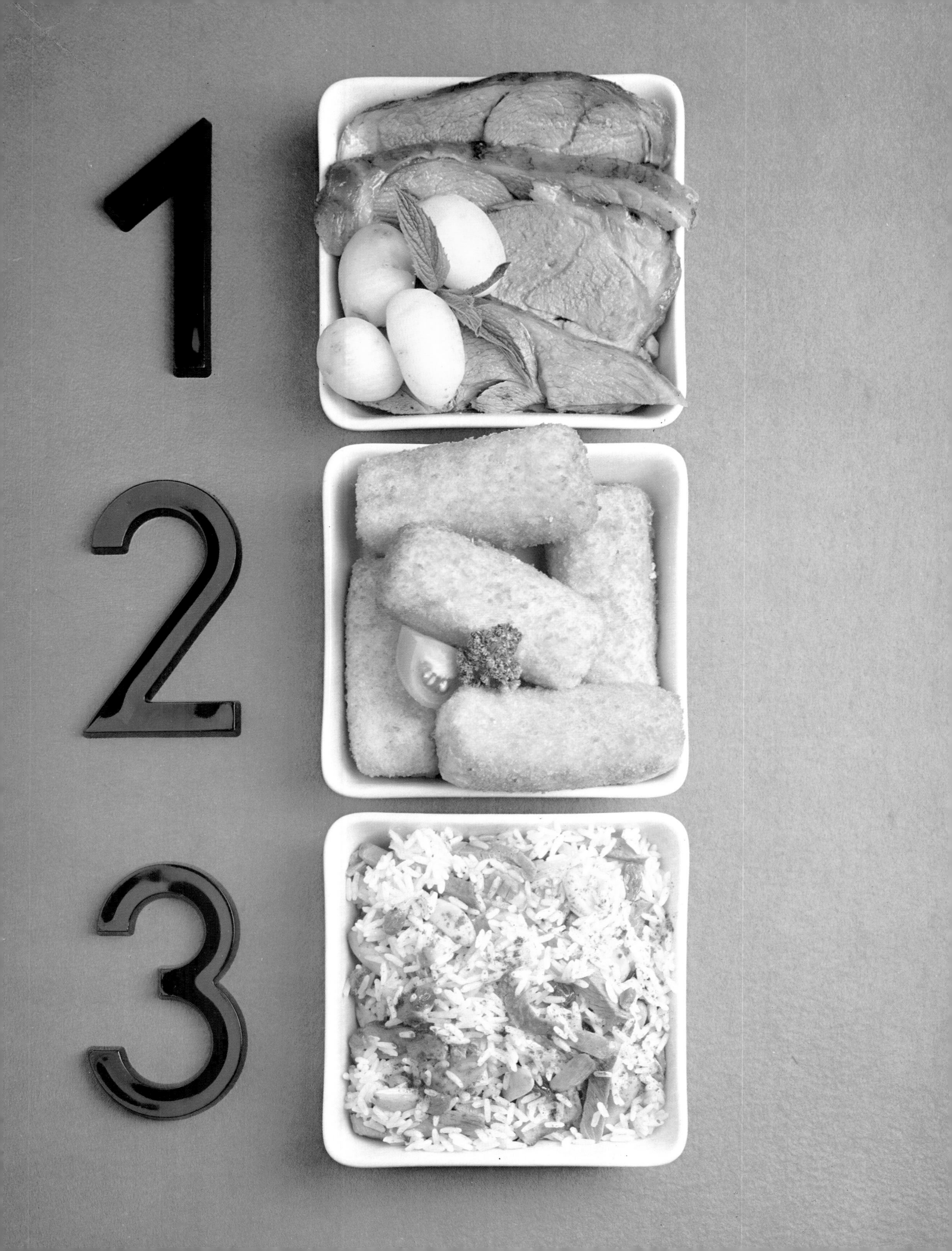
1
2
3

A TURKEY FOR THREE MEALS

1. Roast Stuffed Turkey with Cranberry Sauce

☆ ☆ ① ① ① ✕ ✕ ✕

Preparation and cooking time:
about 3¼ hours

1 x 2.75 kg/6 lb oven-ready turkey
25 g/1 oz butter
salt
freshly ground black pepper
For the apricot stuffing:
50 g/2 oz dried apricots, soaked
   overnight
50 g/2 oz fresh white breadcrumbs
1.25 ml/¼ teaspoon mixed spice
salt and freshly ground black pepper
10 ml/2 teaspoons lemon juice
15 ml/1 tablespoon melted butter
1 small egg, beaten
For the chestnut stuffing:
750 g/1½ lb chestnuts, peeled and
   skinned
turkey or chicken stock (basic recipe)
25 g/1 oz butter
salt and freshly ground black pepper
For the cranberry sauce:
225 g/8 oz cranberries
150 ml/5 fl oz water
50-100 g/2-4 oz sugar, to taste
a little dry sherry or dry vermouth

Heat the oven to 450°F (Gas Mark 8, 230°C).
Drain any moisture from the bird and wipe dry, inside and out. Make giblet stock for the gravy. Note the oven-ready weight of the bird.
Then prepare the apricot stuffing. Drain the liquid from the apricots. Chop the fruit and stir in the breadcrumbs, spice, salt, pepper, lemon juice and melted butter. Bind with the beaten egg.
Free the skin from the turkey breast.
Gently push the apricot mixture under the loosened breast skin, pushing down and over the sides of the breast, so that it will keep the meat moist during cooking. Neatly secure the neck skin with skewers.
Next, cook the prepared chestnuts in boiling stock, or salted water, for 20 minutes or until tender. Drain them thoroughly and toss them with butter, salt and freshly ground black

pepper. Stuff the body cavity loosely with the chestnuts, and close the vent with a skewer.
Brush the bird with softened butter and season with salt and freshly ground black pepper. Prick the breast skin all over—this prevents it bursting as the stuffing swells. Then, either wrap the bird loosely in aluminium foil and place in a roasting tin breast down, or put the bird directly onto the rack in the roasting tin, (again breast down) and cover with foil, folding the edges over the lip of the tin.
Roast the bird for 2-2½ hours, turning it halfway through the cooking time. Test by piercing the thickest part of the leg with a skewer: if the juices run clear the bird is cooked. Any pinkness means that additional cooking time is necessary.
While the turkey is cooking, prepare the cranberry sauce. Stew the cranberries in the water until they 'pop', adding more water if necessary. Rub the fruit through a nylon sieve. Sweeten to taste and re-heat, adding a little sherry or dry vermouth if you wish.

2. Turkey Divan

☆ ① ①

Preparation and cooking time:
45 minutes

350 g/12 oz cooked turkey, diced
225 g/8 oz frozen broccoli
45 ml/3 tablespoons grated Parmesan
1 packet savoury white sauce mix
300 ml/10 fl oz milk
45 ml/3 tablespoons dry sherry
2 egg yolks
45 ml/3 tablespoons double
   cream
salt and freshly ground black pepper

Heat the oven to 350°F (Gas Mark 4, 180°C).
Cook the broccoli according to the instructions on the packet. Drain thoroughly and arrange in the base of a casserole. Sprinkle with 15 ml/1 tablespoon of grated Parmesan.
Make up the sauce according to the instructions on the packet, using

the milk. Remove from the heat.
Mix the sherry, egg yolks and cream in a small bowl, then stir them into the white sauce. Add 15 ml/1 tablespoon Parmesan. Taste and season the sauce with salt and pepper.
Spoon half the sauce over the broccoli. Arrange the turkey on top and cover with the remaining sauce. Sprinkle the last tablespoon of grated Parmesan on top.
Bake for 30 minutes or until the dish is hot right through and the sauce is bubbling and golden.

3. Turkey in Wine Sauce

☆ ① ①

Preparation and cooking time:
55 minutes

25 g/1 oz dripping
25 g/1 oz flour
300 ml/10 fl oz turkey stock
salt and freshly ground black pepper
40 g/1½ oz butter
350 g/12 oz sliced turkey
1 small onion, chopped
5 ml/1 teaspoon dried tarragon
30 ml/2 tablespoons chopped parsley
30 ml/2 tablespoons dry red wine
half a lemon

Melt the dripping in a saucepan and stir in the flour. Cook over low heat for about 15-20 minutes until the roux is cooked to a deep golden brown. Gradually add the stock, stirring vigorously all the while to prevent lumps from forming. Bring to the boil and simmer for 2-3 minutes. Taste and season with salt and pepper.
In a frying pan, heat the butter and sauté the sliced turkey until well heated through. Drain the turkey well and place on a heated serving dish and keep warm.
Fry the chopped onion in the fat remaining in the pan. When soft and golden add it to the turkey sauce. Bring the sauce to the boil and add the tarragon, parsley and wine. Taste and flavour with lemon juice, salt and pepper. Pour the sauce over the turkey slices, garnish with lemon and serve.

EXCITING VEGETABLES

There are plenty of legitimate excuses for not cooking complicated or elaborate main dishes every day of the week. But although you may have to resort to quick stand-bys like chops, steaks or grills these can often be made a lot more interesting by serving them with imaginatively cooked vegetables.

Creamed Potatoes with Spring Onions

☆　　①　　⊠

Preparation and cooking time: *35 minutes*

350 g/12 oz potatoes
salt
1 bunch spring onions
　cleaned
40 g/1½ butter
15 ml/1 tablespoon single cream
freshly ground black pepper

Peel and cut the potatoes into even-sized pieces, then cook in boiling salted water for 25-30 minutes. *Meanwhile* chop up the spring onions finely. Melt the butter in a saucepan, add the onions and cook for 10-15 minutes until soft.
Drain and mash the potatoes, at the same time adding the spring onions and the butter in which they were cooked. Mash in the cream and season with salt and pepper. Spoon into a warmed serving dish and serve.

Left: Buttered Cauliflower with Nutmeg, Spiced Red Cabbage with Apples, Courgettes with Tomatoes, Brussels Sprouts with Chestnuts

Brussels Sprouts with Chestnuts

☆ ▨

Preparation and cooking time:
12 minutes

**225 g/8 oz Brussels sprouts, cleaned
   and trimmed**
**100g/4 oz canned, whole,
   unsweetened chestnuts**
40 g/1½ oz butter
freshly ground black pepper

Cook the cleaned brussels sprouts in
boiling salted water for 5-6 minutes
or until cooked but still firm. Drain
well.
Drain the chestnuts, cut them into
halves and sauté in butter for 2-3
minutes.
Add the brussels sprouts to the
chestnuts and continue cooking for 1
minute over low heat, shaking the pan
to coat everything with the butter.
Season with pepper.

Spiced Red Cabbage

☆

Preparation and cooking time:
2 hours 10 minutes
This will provide enough for 2 meals
for 2 people.

450 g/1 lb red cabbage
25 g/1 oz butter
1 small onion, chopped
**225 g/8 oz cooking apples, peeled,
   cored and chopped**
salt and freshly ground black pepper
freshly grated nutmeg
30ml/2 tablespoons water
30 ml/2 tablespoons wine vinegar
10 ml/2 teaspoons brown sugar

Heat the oven to 300°F (Gas Mark 2,
150°C).
Discard the outer leaves of the
cabbage, cut it into quarters and
remove the stalk, wash and shred
finely.

Melt the butter and fry the onions
until softened. Add the apples and
cook for 1-2 minutes.
Into a casserole put first a layer of
cabbage, then a layer of the onion
and apple mixture and season well
with salt, pepper and plenty of
nutmeg. Continue adding alternate
layers until all the vegetables and fruit
are in the casserole.
Add the water, wine vinegar and
brown sugar. Cover with a lid and
cook in the oven for 2 hours.

Courgettes with Tomatoes

☆   ▨

Preparation and cooking time:
25 minutes

225g/8 oz small courgettes
15 ml/1 tablespoon olive oil
1 garlic clove, crushed
**100 g/4 oz tomatoes, skinned and
   chopped**
salt
freshly ground black pepper

Wipe the courgettes with a damp
cloth and cut them into rounds
about 1 cm/¼ inch thick. Sauté
them very gently in olive oil for 10-15
minutes, turning them over now and
then, until they are soft. Add the
crushed garlic and chopped
tomatoes and cook for a further 6 or
7 minutes.
Season with salt and freshly ground
black pepper.

Buttered Cauliflower

☆

Preparation and cooking time:
10-15 minutes

1 small cauliflower
1 bay leaf

freshly grated nutmeg
25 g/1 oz butter
freshly ground black pepper

Wash the cauliflower, cut off the
hard stalk at the base and any tough
outer leaves.
Place the cauliflower upright in a
pan with 2.5 cm/1 inch of boiling salted
water. Add the bay leaf and grate
generously with nutmeg all over the
top. Cover the pan with a lid and
simmer for 8-10 minutes or until
the cauliflower is cooked but still
firm (test this with a skewer).
Drain well and melt the butter over
the top. Season with pepper.

New Potatoes with Mint and Chives

☆

Preparation and cooking time:
30 minutes

350 g/12 oz new potatoes
salt
1 large sprig mint
25 g/1 oz butter
10 ml/2 teaspoons chopped mint
10 ml/2 teaspoons chopped chives
freshly ground black pepper

Wash the potatoes, but do not peel
them. Place them in a pan, pour
boiling water over them, salt and a
sprig of mint. Cover and cook for
20-25 minutes, or until cooked
through but still firm.
Drain the potatoes. Add the butter,
chopped mint and chives, and shake
the pan to get each potato well
covered with the butter and herbs.
Season with freshly ground pepper.

POULTRY

Roast Stuffed Spring Chicken

Preparation and cooking time:
1 hour 40 minutes

1 x 750 g/1½ lb chicken, with giblets
25 g/1 oz softened butter
For the stuffing:
50 g/2 oz stale white breadcrumbs
60 ml/4 tablespoons milk
**15 g/½ oz butter, at room
    temperature**
1 egg, separated
liver from the chicken
**45 ml/3 tablespoons fresh dill, finely
    chopped**
salt and freshly ground black pepper

Heat the oven to 350°F (Gas Mark 4,
150°C).
Wipe the chicken clean, inside and
out. Put the liver aside until needed.
Put the breadcrumbs in a bowl, add
the milk and leave to soak for 15
minutes. In a mixing bowl, beat the
softened butter and egg yolk.
Chop the chicken liver coarsely.
Squeeze the surplus milk from the
breadcrumbs, combine with the
chicken liver and pass through the
fine blade of a mincer.
Blend the breadcrumb mixture with
butter and egg yolk. Then add the
finely chopped dill and season well
with salt and pepper.
Whisk the egg white until stiff, but
not dry and fold into the stuffing.
Loosen the skin all over the breast
of the chicken carefully easing your
hand between the skin and breast
meat. Take care not to tear skin.
Push the stuffing between the skin
and the breast meat, covering the
entire breast with an even, thin layer.
Fill the cavity of the bird with any
remaining stuffing. Skewer the cavity
together, making sure that the stuffing
cannot run out from under the breast
skin. Truss the chicken.
Melt the butter in a small roasting
tin. When it is hot, turn the chicken
over in the butter to coat it
thoroughly; then lay it breast down
on a rack in the tin. Roast the chicken
basting frequently for about 1 hour,
until the juices run clear when a
skewer is pushed through the
thickest part of the leg.
To serve the chicken, remove it from
the roasting tin and slice it in half
down the middle. Place the 2 halves
on a heated serving dish, side by side
to reform the original chicken shape.

Duck with Turnips

Preparation and cooking time:
about 2¾ hours

450 g/1 lb young turnips
1 small oven-ready duck
salt
freshly ground black pepper
flour
25 g/1 oz butter
10 ml/2 teaspoons caster sugar
425 ml/15 fl oz chicken stock
a bouquet garni
1 medium-sized onion, quartered

Peel and quarter the turnips. Place
them in a saucepan. Cover with cold
water, add salt, then bring to the boil
and simmer for 5 minutes. Drain well.
Wipe the duck clean inside and out.
Rub all over with salt and pepper and
dust with a little flour. In a heavy
casserole large enough to take the
duck and turnips comfortably, heat
the butter. Brown the duck thoroughly
on all sides, then lift it out of the
casserole and keep warm. Now put the
drained turnips into the casserole,
sprinkle them with sugar and sauté
for 3-4 minutes or until lightly
coloured, then lift them out of the
casserole and set aside for later use.
Blend 15 ml/1 tablespoon flour into the
fat left in the casserole, cook for 2-3
minutes, then gradually add the
chicken stock, stirring constantly.
Bring to the boil, stirring. Add the
bouquet garni and quartered onion,
and season to taste with salt and
pepper.
Return the duck to the casserole and
spoon the sauce over the top. Cover
tightly and simmer *very* gently for 1½
hours, turning the duck occasionally
so that it cooks evenly.
Add the sautéed turnips to the
casserole and continue to simmer for
a further 30-40 minutes, or until
both the duck and turnips are tender.
When cooked, transfer the duck to a
heated serving dish; surround with the
turnips and keep hot. Skim the sauce
if necessary, then boil briskly for
about 12 minutes or until reduced to
nearly one-third the original
quantity. Strain a little sauce over the
duck and turnips and serve the rest
in a sauce-boat.

Chicken in Cider

Preparation and cooking time:
1¼ hours

a little oil and butter, for frying
4 small chicken pieces
1 medium-sized onion, chopped
1 garlic clove, crushed
4 slices streaky bacon, chopped
100 g/4 oz mushrooms, sliced
1.25 ml/¼ teaspoon dried thyme
salt and freshly ground black pepper
freshly ground black pepper
425 ml/15 fl oz dry cider
15 g/½ oz butter
15 ml/1 tablespoon flour

Melt some oil and butter in a large
frying pan and fry the chicken pieces
until golden on all sides. Using a
perforated spoon, transfer the chicken
pieces to an flame-proof casserole.
In the same frying pan (adding a
little more oil and butter if
necessary) gently fry the onion,
garlic and chopped bacon for about
10 minutes. Again using a perforated
spoon, arrange them over the chicken
pieces in the casserole.
Toss the mushrooms in the frying pan
over low heat for a minute or two,
then add them to the casserole with
the thyme, bay leaf and seasoning.
Pour the cider into the casserole,
bring to simmering point on top of
the stove, then cover with a lid and
simmer very gently for about 45
minutes or until the chicken is tender.
When the chicken is cooked, transfer
it to a warmed serving dish with the
bacon and vegetables and keep warm.
Work the butter and flour to a smooth
paste, then break it up into
peanut-sized pieces, add them to the
cooking liquid and bring it slowly
back to simmering point, by which
time the butter and flour will have
melted and thickened the sauce.
Taste to check the seasoning, then
pour over the chicken. Serve with rice.

Opposite: Chicken in Cider

MAIN MEALS WITH GAME

Casserole of Rabbit

✡ ✡ ⊕ ⊕ ⊠ ⊠

Preparation and cooking time:
2 hours

4 rabbit pieces
75 g/3 oz caster sugar
25 g/1 oz butter
30 ml/ 2 tablespoon oil
600 ml/1 pint stock (basic recipe)
1 medium-sized onion, thinly sliced
3 slices streaky bacon, cut into
   strips
15 ml/1 tablespoon flour
10 ml/ 2 teaspoons tomato purée
1 strip orange peel
1 garlic clove, crushed
a bouquet garni
salt and freshly ground black pepper
100 g/4 oz button mushrooms, thinly
   sliced
8-10 pitted olives, halved
30 ml/2 tablespoons double cream
30 ml/2 tablespoons dry Madeira
30 ml/2 tablespoon chopped parsley

Roll each rabbit piece in caster
sugar. Heat half each of the
butter and oil in a deep frying pan,
then sauté the rabbit in the hot fat
until the sugar has caramelized.
Remove the rabbit pieces from the
pan and pour in half the measured
stock. Bring to the boil, scraping
the base and sides of the pan.
Replace the rabbit pieces in the pan,
cover and put to one side.
Heat the remaining butter and oil in
a flame-proof casserole and sauté the
onion and bacon until the bacon is
crisp and the onions golden. Stir in
the flour and cook over low heat
until the flour has browned. Pour in
the remaining stock and bring to the
boil, stirring all the time. Add the
tomato purée, orange peel, crushed
garlic and bouquet garni. Season
with a little salt and pepper. Then add
the rabbit joints and their juices.
Place a sheet of greaseproof or waxed
paper on top of the contents of the
casserole, and cover with a well-
fitting lid.
Bring to the boil, then cook very
gently for about 1½ hours. 30 minutes
before the end of the cooking
time, add the sliced mushrooms.
When the rabbit meat is tender, lift
the pieces from the sauce with a
perforated spoon, place them in a
warmed serving dish, cover and keep
hot.
Remove the orange peel and bouquet
garni and add the olives. Bring the
sauce to the boil, then remove from
the heat and stir in the cream and
Madeira. Taste and season with a
little extra salt if necessary. Pour the
sauce over the rabbit pieces and
garnish with chopped parsley.

Pheasant in Red Wine

✡ ⊕ ⊕ ⊕ ⊠ ⊠

Preparation and cooking time:
about 1¾ hours
The cooking time given below is for
a young pheasant. If the bird you
buy is considerably older, or of
dubious age, as much as 2 hours
cooking may be necessary to tenderize
the meat.

1 small pheasant, trussed
salt and freshly ground black pepper
1 small onion, finely chopped
40 g/1½ oz butter
15 ml/1 tablespoon olive oil
300 ml/10 fl oz Burgundy
10 ml/2 teaspoon flour
8 shallots
15 ml/1 tablespoon sugar
8 button mushrooms
chicken stock (basic recipe)

Heat the oven to 275°F (Gas Mark 1,
140°C).
Season the bird inside and out with
salt and pepper. Stuff the body
cavity with the liver and onion.
Heat together 15 ml/1 tablespoon each
butter and oil. Brown the pheasant
all over thoroughly then transfer to
an oven-proof casserole. Cover and
keep warm.
Add the wine to the frying pan. Bring
it to the boil, stirring and scraping
with a wooden spoon. Boil until the
wine is reduced by half. Remove
from the heat.
Mix the flour together with half a
tablespoon of butter. Add this to the
reduced wine in small pieces, stirring
until dissolved. Return the pan to
the heat and bring to the boil.
Simmer, stirring all the time, for 2-3
minutes until the sauce has thickened.
Pour over the pheasant, cover and
set aside.
Simmer the shallots for 10 minutes in
salted water. Drain thoroughly, then
add 15 ml/1 tablespoon butter to pan
and melt, before adding the sugar.
Sauté the shallots until glazed dark
brown. Turn the contents of the pan
into the pheasant casserole, and add
the button mushrooms. Place the
casserole over heat, bring to
simmering point, cover with a well-
fitting lid and transfer to the oven.
Bake the pheasant for 40-50 minutes
or until tender, basting occasionally.
Add a little stock if the sauce
evaporates too quickly.

Fruited Partridge

✡ ✡ ⊕ ⊕ ⊕ ⊠

Preparation and cooking time:
35 minutes

75 g/3 oz cream cheese
salt and freshly ground black pepper
1 young, oven-ready partridge
40 g/1½ butter
15 ml/1 tablespoon olive oil
2 dessert apples, peeled, cored and
   diced
175 g/6 oz grapes, halved and seeded
30 ml/2 tablespoons brandy

Heat the oven to 450°F (Gas Mark 8,
230°C).
Mix the cheese with salt and pepper
to taste, and stuff the partridge with
the mixture. Truss the bird.
Heat 15 ml/1 tablespoon each butter and
oil in a casserole just large enough
to take the partridge comfortably.
Brown evenly over moderate heat.
Transfer the casserole to the oven and
roast uncovered for 10 minutes.
Meanwhile, melt the remaining butter
in a small pan and toss the diced
apple in it over high heat until golden
but not soft. Remove the casserole
from the oven, cover the partridge
with the apples and grapes and
sprinkle on the brandy. Cover the
casserole with a lid and return it to
the oven for a further 10 minutes.

Opposite: Casserole of Rabbit

FROZEN FISH

Marinated Kippers

Preparation and cooking time:
10 minutes plus 2 weeks or more
After marinating these kippers will taste as good as smoked salmon.

**2 large frozen kippers
or 4 frozen kipper fillets, thawed
1 Spanish onion,
coarsely chopped
300 ml/10 fl oz olive oil**

Fillet and skin the thawed kippers. Lay two fillets side by side at the bottom of a china dish. Cover with chopped onion and top with the remaining fillets. Pour on enough oil to cover the kippers completely, then cover the dish with a well-fitting lid.
Leave the dish at the bottom of the refrigerator for a minimum of 2 weeks, preferably longer.
When ready to serve, drain the fillets and serve with thickly sliced brown bread and butter.

Trout with Almonds

Preparation and cooking time:
20 minutes
Here is another very quick and simple fish dish. But take care when frying the almonds—watch them all the time because they brown very easily.

**2 frozen trout, thawed
salt
freshly ground black pepper
a little milk
a little flour
50 g/2 oz butter
10 ml/2 teaspoons olive oil
60 ml/4 tablespoons flaked almonds
the juice of half a lemon
30 ml/2 tablespoons finely chopped
parsley**

Season the trout with salt and black pepper. Dip them in milk, then in flour, shaking off the excess afterwards.
In a frying pan melt half the butter with the olive oil. Fry the fish until they are golden brown on both sides and the flesh flakes off easily with a fork—about 4-5 minutes on each side. Remove the fish from the pan and place on a heated serving dish.
Drain the fat from the pan and add the remaining butter. When it has melted, add the flaked almonds and fry, shaking the pan, until the almonds are golden brown. Sprinkle with lemon juice and stir in the chopped parsley. Pour the butter juices and almonds over the trout and serve immediately.

Haddock with Prawn and Mushroom Sauce

Preparation and cooking time:
15 minutes
The fact that it is not necessary to thaw the haddock fillets before cooking them makes this a marvellously speedy recipe—about 15 minutes from start to finish.

**350 g/12 oz frozen haddock fillets
salt
freshly ground black pepper
25 g/1 oz butter
10 ml/2 teaspoons oil
100 g/4 oz button mushrooms, thinly
sliced
a squeeze of lemon juice
50 g/2 oz frozen prawns or shrimps
90 ml/6 tablespoons double cream**

Season the haddock fillets with salt and pepper. Melt the butter and oil in a frying pan. Then fry the fillets gently in the hot fat, 4-5 minutes on each side. Transfer the cooked fillets to a heated serving dish and keep hot in a low oven.
Add the sliced mushrooms to the butter remaining in the pan, sprinkle with a little lemon juice and sauté gently for about 3 minutes. Add the prawns or shrimps to the pan and continue to sauté for about 3 minutes more, until heated through. Stir in the cream and simmer very gently until the sauce is heated through and slightly thickened.
Taste and add more seasoning or lemon juice if necessary.
Spoon the sauce over the haddock fillets. Garnish each fillet with a slice of lemon, and sprinkle with finely chopped parsley.

Fried Whitebait

Preparation and cooking time:
15-20 minutes
This dish is suitable as a fish course, or as a main dish for lunch or supper. The *whole* fish is eaten. so do not let anyone tell you otherwise! It is important to get the fish absolutely dry before lightly and singly flouring each one.

**225 g/8 oz whitebait, thawed
seasoned flour
salt
cayenne pepper
sprigs of parsley
wedges of lemon**

Rinse the whitebait thoroughly, then drain well and dry them on absorbent kitchen paper. Toss the fish gently in seasoned flour, making sure each fish is individually and evenly coated. Shake off any surplus flour.
Heat a pan of deep oil to 370°F (180°C). Make sure you use a frying basket with a fine mesh. Fry the whitebait, a small handful at a time, for 2-3 minutes until crisply cooked. Shake the basket from time to time to keep the fish separate.
Drain the cooked whitebait well, turning them onto absorbent kitchen paper; keep hot on a serving dish until they are all fried.
Serve the fish sprinkled with salt and cayenne pepper and garnished with wedges of lemon and sprigs of parsley.

Opposite: Fried Whitebait

FRESH FISH

Sole with Creamy Sauce and Iced Grapes

 ① ① ① ▨

Preparation and cooking time:
45 minutes
The grapes in this recipe can be served hot should you prefer. If so, heat them in a little fish stock or white wine just before serving.

1 x 750 g/1½ lb sole
425 ml/15 fl oz water
150 ml/5 fl oz dry white wine
3 or 4 black peppercorns
salt
1 small onion, peeled and quartered
1 small bayleaf
a few parsley stalks
25 g/1 oz butter
45 ml/3 tablespoons flour
45 ml/3 tablespoons double cream
paprika
75 g/3 oz white grapes, peeled, halved, seeded and chilled

Remove the head from the sole, then skin and fillet the fish. Place the washed head, skin and bones (broken up) in a pan with the water, wine, peppercorns, a little salt, the onion, bayleaf and parsley stalks. Bring slowly to the boil and simmer uncovered for 15-20 minutes or until the liquid is reduced to about 300 ml/10 fl oz. Strain the stock and reserve.
Season the fillets, then fold each in half, skin side inside. Place in a small greased, flame-proof casserole, pour on the fish stock and poach over low heat for 10-15 minutes. Then strain off the poaching liquid and keep the fillets hot in the covered dish.
Melt the butter in a saucepan and stir in the flour. Cook for a few minutes before adding the strained

Opposite top: Herrings in Oatmeal; below: Grilled Mackerel with Gooseberry Sauce

poaching liquid. Bring the sauce to the boil slowly and simmer for 2-3 minutes, stirring all the time.
Remove the pan from the heat and stir in enough cream to give the sauce a coating consistency. Season to taste. Coat the fillets with the sauce and garnish with a light dusting of paprika.
Serve the sole sprinkled with the chilled grapes.

Herrings in Oatmeal

 ① ▨

Preparation and cooking time:
15 minutes
Herrings are never better than when simply prepared, as here—just coated with oatmeal and fried, in the Scottish style. Medium ground or fine oatmeal is traditional, but rolled (porridge) oats can be used if crushed first. Place them in a plastic bag and crush with a rolling pin.

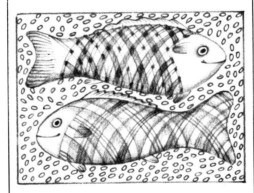

2 medium-sized herrings
45 ml/3 tablespoons oatmeal
2.5 ml/½ teaspoon salt
15 g/½ oz butter
15 ml/1 tablespoon oil
lemon wedges
parsley

Remove the heads from the herrings and scrape the skin from head to tail. to remove the scales. Rinse well and dry with absorbent kitchen paper. Cut along the underside of each fish, remove the roe and reserve for serving separately. Scrape away and discard the gut.
Open out each fish and place it skin side uppermost on a board. Press along the back of the fish to loosen the back bone. Turn it over and gently ease away the backbone, starting at

the head end. Cut off the fins.
Mix the oatmeal and salt on a large plate and dip in each fish to coat thoroughly on both sides. Melt the butter and oil in a frying pan and fry the herring for 5-8 minutes, turning the fish once half way through the cooking time.
Drain the fish on absorbent kitchen paper and serve immediately on a warmed serving dish with a garnish of lemon wedges and sprigs of parsley.

Grilled Mackerel with Gooseberry Sauce

 ① ▨

Preparation and cooking time:
about 30 minutes
This recipe seems to be peculiar to England. It is one of those unlikely-sounding combinations which taste extremely good.

225 g/8 oz young gooseberries
15 g/½ oz butter
sugar, to taste
2 mackerel
lemon juice
salt
freshly ground black pepper
cooking oil

Top and tail the gooseberries. Wash them, then place them in a small saucepan with just enough water to cover. Simmer gently until cooked.
Drain the gooseberries and rub the pulp through a sieve. Mix the gooseberry purée with the butter and sugar to taste. Keep hot in a sauceboat whilst preparing the mackerel.
Pre-heat the grill.
Gut the mackerel and remove the head and fins. Wash and wipe dry, then season the fish inside and out with lemon juice, salt and pepper. Score each fish lightly on both sides with 2 oblique cuts.
Place on a foil-lined grill rack and brush with a little oil.
Grill fish under moderate heat until lightly browned. Turn the mackerel, brush with oil and brown on the other side.
Serve the fish immediately they are cooked and accompany with the gooseberry sauce.

Left top: Fresh Lemon Jelly
Bottom: Treacle Tart
Below left: Cream Cup Dessert
Right: Apricot Cinnamon Crumble

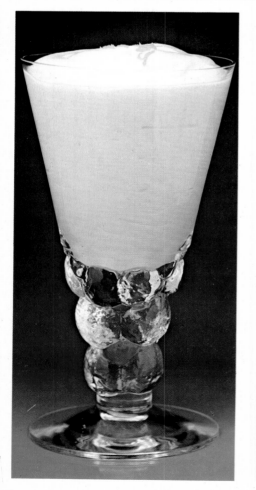

DESSERTS

Treacle Tart

Preparation and cooking time:
30 minutes
There are, in fact, lots of ways of ringing the changes with this old English favourite. For example you could use crushed cornflakes or shredded wheat instead of white breadcrumbs. Then again, you could use orange instead of lemon, sprinkling a little grated zest over the syrup topping for extra flavour.

175 g/6 oz shortcrust pastry
40 g/1½ oz fresh white breadcrumbs
10 ml/2 teaspoons lemon juice
60 ml/4 tablespoons golden syrup

Heat the oven to 425°F (Gas Mark 7, 220°C).
Roll out the pastry to line a 20 cm/8-inch oven-proof plate and overlap the rim of the plate by 1.5 cm/½ inch. Turn the overlapping pastry under to give a double thickness around the rim. Pinch the edges together to decorate.
Sprinkle the breadcrumbs over the pastry followed by lemon juice, then drizzle the syrup on top.
Bake in the centre of the oven for 20-25 minutes until golden brown.
Serve hot or cold with custard or cream.

Lemon Sponge Pudding

Preparation and cooking time: *1¼ hours*
This pudding has an apparently disastrous curdled appearance before it goes into the oven. But do not worry: it will separate into a delightful sponge-topped pudding with a delicious lemony sauce underneath.

50 g/2 oz butter at room temperature
100 g/4 oz caster sugar
the grated zest and juice of 2 lemons
2 egg, separated
50 g/2 oz flour, sifted
a pinch of salt
150 ml/5 fl oz milk

Heat the oven to 350°F (Gas Mark 4, 180°C).
Cream the butter, sugar and grated lemon zest until light and fluffy. Beat in the egg yolks, then fold in the flour and salt a little at a time alternately with tablespoons of milk. Stir in the lemon juice.
In a separate mixing bowl beat the egg whites until stiff but not dry, then fold into the lemon mixture. Pour the mixture into a small pie dish.
Place the pie dish in a small roasting tin and pour enough water into the tin to come halfway up the side of the pie dish. Bake for 50-60 minutes until the top is well-risen and golden.
Serve immediately, sprinkling the top with a little caster sugar.

Pineapple Waffles

Preparation and cooking time:
15-20 minutes
Waffles are very quick and easy to make. That makes them marvellous for an emergency dessert. Heat the pineapple juice from the can to make an accompanying syrup.

75 g/3 oz flour
a pinch of salt
7.5 ml/1½ teaspoons baking powder
15 ml/1 tablespoon caster sugar
1 egg, separated
150 ml/5 fl oz. milk
30 ml/2 tablespoons melted butter
a few drops of vanilla essence
50 g/2 oz drained canned pineapple, chopped

Sift the flour, salt and baking powder into a mixing bowl and stir in the sugar. Make a well in the centre and add the egg yolk. Mix it in, alternately adding a little milk and melted butter. Then stir in the vanilla essence.
In a separate bowl beat the egg whites until stiff but not dry, and fold lightly into the mixture, together with the chopped pineapple.
Heat the waffle iron and pour a little batter on to it. Cook on both sides for a total of 2-3 minutes. Transfer to a warm serving dish to keep hot while making the rest of the waffles.
Serve as soon as possible with hot pineapple syrup.

Cream Cup Dessert

Preparation time:
15 minutes, plus 5 hours
In this recipe the maceration time given is the absolute minimum. The flavour is improved if the bowl is left covered in a cool place overnight. Don't worry too much about the quality of the wine—one of the cheaper brands of dry white wine from a supermarket will be quite all right.

60 ml/4 tablespoons dry white wine
15 ml/1 tablespoon lemon juice
5 ml/1 teaspoon finely grated lemon zest
40 g/1½ oz caster sugar
150 ml/5 fl oz double cream

Put the wine, lemon juice and zest, and sugar into a bowl. Cover and leave for at least 3 hours.
Pour the cream onto the wine and lemon mixture, then beat until the mixture will hold a shape.
Transfer the mixture to small serving glasses—wine glasses will do—and leave in a cool place for a few hours before serving.

Pears with Chocolate Sauce

Preparation and cooking time:
30 minutes plus 2 hours
Increase the quantities to make a delicious and spectacular party piece.

2 ripe dessert pears
300 ml/10 fl oz water
50 g/2 oz caster sugar
1 vanilla pod
2 cloves
For the chocolate sauce:
100 g/4 oz plain chocolate, broken up into small squares
30 ml/2 tablespoons of water
15 g/½ oz unsalted butter
15 ml/1 tablespoon double cream

Peel the pears, leaving the stalks on; remove the 'eye' from underneath and slice a little off so that the pears will sit upright.
Place the sugar, water, vanilla and cloves in a small saucepan and dissolve the sugar over low heat, then boil rapidly for 1 minute.
Place the pears upright in the syrup and poach them for 15-20 minutes, then lift them out with a perforated spoon and place on a serving dish. Cool and chill thoroughly.
Just before serving, place the chocolate and water in a small bowl fitted over a pan of simmering water. When the chocolate has melted, add the butter and cream and beat till smooth.
Pour the sauce over the pears and serve at once. Fan-shaped wafers or *langue du chat* biscuits, make a nice accompaniment.

Fresh Lemon Jelly

Preparation and cooking time:
30 minutes plus 2¼ hours
We have become so conditioned to shop-bought products nowadays that we forget just what the real thing tastes like (custard, for example, mayonnaise, and tomato soup). Here is a chance to make a real jelly

Left: Pears with Chocolate Sauce

and taste for yourself—then surely you'll never use a commercial jelly again.

3 lemons
1 small pieces of cinnamon stick
1 clove
300 ml/10 fl oz water
25 ml/1½ tablespoons powdered gelatine
75 g/3 oz sugar, or to taste
a few frosted grapes

Using a potato peeler, remove only the yellow zest from the lemons, discarding all the white pith as this gives a slightly bitter flavour. Put the lemon zest, cinnamon stick, clove and 150 ml/5 fl oz of the water into a saucepan. Bring slowly to the boil, then remove from the heat, cover and leave to infuse for 10 minutes.
Squeeze the juice from the lemons and strain into a measuring jar (there should be about 150 ml/5 fl oz of juice—if not, squeeze an additional lemon to make up the amount).
Sprinkle gelatine over the infused water and leave for 5 minutes. Add the sugar and stir until dissolved. Stir in the lemon juice and a further 150 ml/5 fl oz of water. Taste, add more sugar if you wish, and stir until quite dissolved. Strain the liquid into a 900 ml/1½ pint jelly mould, and leave in a refrigerator or cool place until set.
To turn out the jelly, dip the mould for 2 seconds in very hot water and invert it onto a plate. Decorate with frosted grapes.

Apricot Cinnamon Crumble

Preparation and cooking time:
55 minutes

175 g/6 oz canned apricots
10 ml/2 teaspoons soft brown sugar
10 ml/2 teaspoons ground cinnamon
2.5 ml/½ teaspoon ground ginger
For the topping:
40 g/1½ oz butter, at room temperature
75 g/3 oz wholemeal flour
15 ml/1 tablespoon rolled oats
30 ml/2 tablespoons soft brown sugar
5 ml/1 teaspoon ground cinnamon

Heat the oven to 350°F (Gas Mark 4, 180°C).
Butter a small baking dish and arrange the apricots in it with about one tablespoon of their syrup. Sprinkle them with soft brown sugar, cinnamon and ground ginger.
Then make the topping: rub the butter into the flour and when it is crumbly, mix in the oats and soft brown sugar.
Arrange the crumble mixture lightly over the apricots, sprinkle a teaspoon of cinnamon on top and bake in the oven for 45 minutes or until the top is golden and crispy.
Serve slightly warm with cream.

Caramelized Peaches and Pears

Preparation and cooking time:
25 minutes

1 large dessert pear
1 large fresh peach
45 ml/3 tablespoons demerara sugar
100 ml/4 fl oz. double cream
10 ml/2 teaspoons caster sugar

Peel and core the pear, and peel and stone the peach. Cut the fruit into bite-size pieces and arrange in a small shallow oven-proof dish. Cover the fruit completely with the demerara sugar and then place the dish in the freezing compartment of the refrigerator for 15 minutes.
Pre-heat the grill to very hot, then place the dish containing the fruit underneath it until the sugar starts to caramelize. Allow to cool, and if made ahead of time, place the dish in the main body of the refrigerator to chill.
Whip the cream lightly with the caster sugar and serve with the caramelized fruit.

LEFTOVERS

Very small quantities of leftover meat or vegetables can always be used for light dishes—to fill vol-au-vent or omelettes—and bones will make good stock. Larger quantities can be used to make delicious and substantial dishes as the following recipes prove!

Spiced Mutton Pie

Preparation and cooking time:
55 minutes

350 g/12 oz cold mutton or lamb, finely chopped
1 medium cooking apple, peeled, cored and finely chopped
10 ml/2 teaspoons caster sugar
4 pitted prunes, chopped
half a whole nutmeg, freshly grated
60 ml/4 tablespoons leftover gravy from roast lamb
salt
freshly ground black pepper
100 g/4 oz flaky or shortcrust pastry
a little milk

Heat the oven to 400°F (Gas Mark 6, 200°C).
Choose a pie dish that is not too large as the ingredients should come a little above the rim. Grease it with a little butter.
Pack in the meat and apples in alternate layers. Season each layer of meat with salt and pepper, and each layer of apples with freshly grated nutmeg and a sprinkling of caster sugar. Add a few pieces of the prunes here and there, and finally pour on the gravy.
Roll out the pastry and cover the pie with it, giving a double layer round the rim. Decorate with the strips left over from the pastry, make a

hole in the centre of the lid, brush the pastry all over with the milk, then bake in the oven for 15 minutes.
Reduce the temperature to 350°F (Gas Mark 4, 180°C) and bake for a further 30 minutes.
Serve with a green vegetable and redcurrant jelly.

Savoury Meat Pie

Preparation and cooking time:
1¼ hours
This is a great pie for using up absolutely all your leftovers! Remember to put all pies onto a baking sheet before they go into the oven as they invariably bubble over during cooking.

50 g/2 oz butter
1 small onion, chopped
1 celery stalk, chopped
45 ml/3 tablespoons flour
425 ml/15 fl oz thin gravy or stock
225 g/8 oz cooked lamb or beef
225 g/8 oz cooked vegetables (e.g. peas, beans, carrots, sweetcorn)
30 ml/2 tablespoons dry red wine
5 ml/1 teaspoon Worcestershire sauce
2.5 ml/½ teaspoon soy sauce
salt
freshly ground black pepper
175 g/6 oz. shortcrust or flaky pastry

Heat the oven to 400°F (Gas Mark 6, 200°C).
Heat the butter in a medium-sized saucepan and sauté the onion and celery over moderate heat for 5 minutes. Stir in the flour and continue to cook over low heat until the flour is a deep golden brown. Gradually add the gravy or stock, stirring quickly. Bring to the boil then simmer uncovered for 10 minutes, stirring occasionally to prevent sticking or burning.
Add the meat and vegetables to the pan then stir in the wine, the Worcestershire and soy sauces and season to taste with salt and pepper. Cook for about 5 minutes until amalgamated. Pour the mixture into a 900 ml/1½ pint pie dish. Cover and leave to cool.
Roll out the pastry to an oblong, 5 cm/2 inches larger than the top of pie dish. Cut off a 1.5 cm/½-inch wide strip from around the edge of the pastry.

Brush the rim of the pie dish with water and press this pastry strip on to the rim. Brush the pastry strip with water and place the remaining pastry in position over the top of the pie. Lightly press the edges together and trim off the excess pastry. Pinch together to seal well.
Re-roll the pastry trimmings and cut out leaves to decorate the top of the pie. Make a steam hole in the centre. Glaze the pie all over with beaten egg and place on a baking sheet.
Bake for 30-40 minutes until the pie is golden brown on top.

Savoury Croquettes

Preparation and cooking time:
30 minutes plus 8 hours
For this recipe, use any stale bread you have left over to make breadcrumbs; they will keep almost indefinitely in a plastic airtight container in the refrigerator. Please don't use shop-bought breadcrumbs, which are little better than bright orange grit!

25 g/1 oz butter
30 ml/2 tablespoons flour
300 ml/10 fl oz plus 30 ml/2 tablespoons milk
350 g/12 oz cooked chicken, finely chopped
50 g/2 oz cooked ham, chopped
30 ml/2 tablespoons grated cheese
2 egg yolks, lightly beaten
salt
freshly ground black pepper
100 g/4 oz fine, stale white breadcrumbs
cooking oil or fat for deep drying

Melt the butter in a medium-sized saucepan and stir in the flour. Cook for 2 minutes over moderate heat. then gradually add 300 ml/10 fl oz of the milk, stirring all the time. Bring slowly to the boil and simmer over low heat for 2-3 minutes, still stirring. Remove the pan from the heat.
Add the chopped chicken and ham, grated Cheddar and lightly beaten egg yolks. Mix well and season to taste

Right: Savoury Meat Pie looks delicious with a beaten egg glaze.
Above: Savoury Croquettes.

with salt and freshly ground black pepper.

Spread the mixture on to a plate. Cover and leave to get cold, preferably overnight in a refrigerator. *When* cold and set, divide the mixture into 8 equal portions. Roll into neat sausage shapes.

Beat egg and 30 ml/2 tablespoons of milk together in a shallow dish. Dust each croquette with flour, then dip in the beaten egg mixture. Drain well then coat in breadcrumbs.

Heat a pan of fat to 375°F (190°C) and deep-fry the croquettes for about 3 minutes. Drain on absorbent kitchen paper and serve immediately.

Crisp Pancake Rolls

Preparation and cooking time:
about 30 minutes
The pancakes can be prepared in advance and stored in layers, between oiled sheets of greaseproof or waxed paper, in a refrigerator. Stored this way they will keep for up to a week. Leftover duck, turkey, partridge or rabbit could equally well be used in place of chicken.

**6 pancakes, about 15 cm/6 in across
    (basic recipe)**
1 egg
**75 g/3 oz fine, stale white
    breadcrumbs**
40 g/1½ oz butter
45 ml/3 tablespoons olive oil
For the filling:
**1 medium-sized onion,
    finely chopped**
15 ml/1 tablespoon olive oil
**175 g/6 oz cooked chicken meat,
    coarsely minced**
30 ml/2 tablespoons chopped parsley
1.25 ml/¼ teaspoon dried mixed herbs
1 egg yolk
30 ml/2 tablespoons double cream
30 ml/2 tablespoons milk
salt
freshly ground black pepper

To make the filling, heat the olive oil in a pan and fry the onion until soft and golden. Remove the onion from the pan and mix with the remaining filling ingredients, adding salt and freshly ground black pepper to taste.

Place a litre of the filling in the centre of a pancake. Fold two sides of the pancake over the filling and roll up into a neat, secure parcel. Repeat with the remaining pancakes.

Beat egg with 15 ml/1 tablespoon of water in a dish. Add a little seasoning. Coat each pancake with beaten egg mixture then coat with breadcrumbs.

Heat equal quantities of butter and oil in a frying pan and fry the pancake rolls for about 8 minutes or until crisp and golden brown on all sides. Drain well and serve immediately.

Moussaka

Preparation and cooking time:
1½ hours

1 large onion, chopped
90 ml/6 tablespoons olive oil
**225 g/8 oz cooked beef or lamb,
    minced**
60 ml/4 tablespoons red wine
15 ml/1 tablespoon tomato purée
**15 ml/1 tablespoon freshly chopped
    parsley**
2.5 ml/½ teaspoon ground cinnamon
salt
freshly ground black pepper
2 medium-sized aubergines
1 large egg
**300 ml/10 fl oz cheese sauce
    (basic recipe)**
a little grated nutmeg

Heat the oven to 350°F (Gas Mark 4, 180°C).

Fry onion in 15 ml/1 tablespoon oil. *In* a small bowl mix the wine, tomato purée, parsley, cinnamon, salt and pepper. Pour the mixture into the frying pan and let it cook gently for 10 minutes. Then add the meat and stir until well mixed.

Slice the aubergines into rounds about 1.5 cm/½-inch thick, and then into halves, without removing the skins. Fry the slices in the remaining oil until lightly browned, then drain them on absorbent paper.

Into a buttered baking-dish put first a layer of aubergines then a layer of the meat mixture. Continue layering in this way until all the ingredients are used up.

Whisk the egg. Make up the cheese sauce, add the egg to it and mix together thoroughly. Add a few gratings of nutmeg, then pour the sauce over the meat and aubergines and bake in the oven for 1 hour.

When cooked the top will have become fluffy and golden brown.

Chicken Risotto

Preparation and cooking time:
50 minutes

75 ml/5 tablespoons oil
**half a green pepper, chopped into
    small pieces**
1 large onion, finely chopped
100 g/4 oz mushrooms
1 chicken liver
350 g/12 oz cooked chicken, diced
salt
freshly ground black pepper
100 g/4 oz long-grain rice
150 ml/5 fl oz hot chicken stock
2 tomatoes, quartered

Heat the oven to 350°F (Gas Mark 4, 180°C).

Heat 60 ml/4 tablespoons oil in a frying pan and fry the green pepper, onion, mushroom stalks and chicken liver. Add the diced chicken and season with salt and pepper.

Then add the rice and stir with a wooden spoon so that it absorbs all the juices.

Transfer the mixture to a casserole and pour on the hot stock.

Stir once, cover closely and bake in the oven for 40-45 minutes.

Meanwhile, sauté the mushroom caps and tomatoes in the remaining oil.

When the risotto is ready, serve it garnished with the mushrooms, tomatoes and a sprinkling of parsley.

BASIC RECIPES

Pilau Rice

25 g/1 oz butter
1 small onion, finely chopped
100 g/4 oz long grain rice
2.5 cm/1 inch cinnamon stick
4 cloves
5 ml/1 teaspoon ground turmeric
1.25 ml/¼ teaspoon ground ginger
350 ml/12 fl oz hot stock
salt and pepper

In a small saucepan melt the butter over gentle heat and cook the onion in it for 5 minutes. Next stir in the rice and the spices.
When everything is well coated with the butter add the stock and a seasoning of salt and pepper.
Stir once, bring to the boil, cover with a lid and simmer very gently for about 25 minutes or until the rice is tender and the liquid is absorbed.
Fluff the rice with a fork before serving.

Fresh Tomato Sauce

225 g/8 oz firm ripe tomatoes
25 ml/1½ tablespoons olive oil
1 small onion, finely chopped
1 very small garlic clove crushed
1.25 ml/¼ teaspoon caster sugar
2.5 ml/½ teaspoon dried basil
salt and pepper

Place the tomatoes in a bowl, pour boiling water over them and leave for 1-2 minutes. Drain and skin the tomatoes and roughly chop the flesh.
Cook the onion in the olive oil over gentle heat for 5 minutes or so, then add the crushed garlic, finely chopped tomatoes, sugar, basil and seasonings. Stir thoroughly, then let the mixture simmer very gently uncovered for approximately 25 minutes
When the sauce is cooked, press it through a fine sieve, reheat and serve.

Pancake Batter

75 g/3 oz flour
a pinch of salt
1 large egg
150 ml/5 fl oz milk
15 ml/1 tablespoon water
15 ml/1 tablespoon melted butter

Sift the flour and salt into a bowl, make a well in the centre and add the egg. Beat the egg, gradually incorporating the flour.
When the mixture begins to stiffen start adding the milk, little by little, beating all the time.
Finally add the water and whisk thoroughly till the mixture is smooth and free of lumps.
The batter can be made in advance, although it is *not* necessary to let it stand for any length of time.
Just before cooking the pancakes, stir in 15 ml/1 tablespoon of melted butter.

Cheese Sauce

65 g/2½ oz butter
half an onion, finely chopped
40 g/1½ oz flour
300 ml/10 fl oz milk
75 g/3 oz grated Cheddar cheese
salt and pepper
a pinch of cayenne

In a small thick based saucepan melt 50 g/2 oz of the butter over gentle heat and cook the onion in it, without browning, for about 6 minutes, then sprinkle in the flour, stir till smooth and add the milk, a little at a time, stirring vigorously after each addition.
When the milk is all blended into the sauce add the cheese and a seasoning of salt, freshly ground black pepper and a pinch of cayenne.
Arrange a few flecks of butter on the surface of the sauce, (but do not stir them into the sauce). Cover with a lid and leave to cook for 8-10 minutes over the lowest heat possible.
Just before serving stir in the remaining amount of butter.

Giblet Stock

the giblets and liver of a chicken,
   turkey or duck
1 small onion, cut in half
1 carrot, sliced in half lengthways
a few parsley stalks
6 black peppercorns
salt to taste
750 ml/1¼ pints water

Place all the ingredients in a saucepan and bring to simmering point.
Spoon off any scum that rises to the surface, then cover with a lid and simmer very gently for 1½-2 hours.
Strain before using.

Cherry Sauce

60 ml/4 tablespoons Morello cherry
   jam
60 ml/4 tablespoons red wine

Using a wooden spoon, combine the two ingredients in a small saucepan and stir over a gentle heat. Bring to simmering point and simmer very gently without a lid for 5 minutes.
This can be made ahead and reheated before serving.
Note: it is important to use Morello cherry jam and no other variety.

ENTERTAINING

All the recipes in this section are for 2 people, but it is relatively easy to double or treble the quantities to serve 4 or 6 for a party. Here are some suggested menus, but of course you can change them around, or make your own selection from the recipes in this book.

Menus

Entertaining is becoming a lot more relaxed nowadays—and the more relaxed *you* are about the whole thing, the better your party is likely to be. Rule number 1 for entertaining is: don't ever try to overstretch yourself financially or physically. The whole idea of a party is that you and your friends should enjoy each other's company while sharing a meal—so don't cut yourself off from the object of the evening by making things difficult for yourself.

Planning the menu

If you have all day to prepare for a dinner party, have the time, and enjoy boning and stuffing a chicken, well and good. But there is no reason why the cook with limited time—because she has a family of small children or a full time job to cope with—should not be able to give an equally successful party.
In this book you will find many recipes which are ideal for the cook who is short of time. There are first course dishes and desserts which can be made well ahead and served cold, and there are main course dishes which positively gain in flavour if prepared in advance and simply reheated when required.

Seasonal variety and value

The taste and flavour of the food are, of course of primary importance and carefully chosen ingredients are paramount.
Nature automatically provides us each month of the year with a perfectly varied diet—and to be interesting food must be varied. So forget about limp imported salads in winter and outrageously expensive summer brussels sprouts, and get to know

when home-grown produce is in season and cheapest.
Search out the very best possible materials and don't be afraid to ask for help and advice. Even if you have to buy eggs, bread and other staple foods from a supermarket, it is well worth finding and making friends with a good butcher, fishmonger and greengrocer.

Attractive presentation

Food must look appetizing too, but that need not involve tomato waterlilies, radish roses, garden peas sitting in nests of mashed potatoes or displays of that sort. Attractive presentation and atmosphere are much more basic, and can turn a simple casserole into an excellent dinner party choice. Simplicity does not, of course, mean lack of style. Attention to detail makes all the difference. A carelessly laid table and a hastily thrown together stew dumped in front of your guests is obviously not condusive to a relaxing and enjoyable evening. However, there's no reason why you shouldn't serve a carefully prepared but simple casserole: if it's presented in a handsome dish it can be most inviting—particularly if you also offer a choice of breads, hot and crusty from the oven, and a selection of ice-cold butters in individual pots (saltless, herb and curry-flavoured butter for example); and follow with a perfectly fresh green mixed salad and a variety of cheeses in peak condition.

The right setting

Experiment with lighting in your dining room—candles can flatter the look of food as well as guests and hostess. Invest in a really nice set of cutlery, glass and china, and add variety with different coloured linen for different occasions. An all-white colour scheme (tablecloth, napkins, flowers and candles) looks cool and elegant in Summer, for example, and deep plum looks warm and welcoming in Winter.

What to drink

If you abide by the generally accepted

rule, you won't go far wrong: white wine with white flesh, red wine with red meat. But further than that, try to match flavours. Lamb, for instance is ideally partnered by a light claret while roast beef can stand up to a richer, full-bodied red Burgundy. Quite simply, the more delicately flavoured the dish, the lighter the wine should be.
You may want to serve a different wine to suit each course. In which case the logical sequence is: white before red, dry before sweet, light before full, young before old. In this way a meal would progress from less interesting wines to those with more flavour— the exception being the sweet dessert wines which are always served at the end of a meal.
If you want to take the easy (and expensive) way out, of course, you can't go wrong by serving champagne throughout the meal—unless the food is highly spiced, in which case any wine is wasted, and beer, cider or a jug of ice cold water with a few lemon slices is the perfect answer.

Convenience Foods

Because of the busy lives so many of us lead today, there is a growing trend towards using more and more convenience foods and—as competition between manufacturers grows increasingly stronger—the quality and range of canned, frozen and other ready-to-eat foods is steadily improving.
Frozen items such as pastry, peas and fish; and canned foods like soups, fruits, tuna fish, salmon and anchovies are stocked in every well-managed kitchen today—not only as insurance against emergency situations but increasingly as part of our daily cooking.
As our recipes show, these mass manufactured foods, if cleverly and carefully used, can prove not merely acceptable but suitable for special occasion cooking.

Bachelor cooking

Having some of the work taken out of cooking is encouraging as well as time and labour saving, particularly

for the novice or occasional cook.
A visit to a good delicatessen can be a rewarding experience for the bachelor who claims he would like—but is unable—to prepare a meal for himself.

In addition to offering a wide range of basic and sophisticated store cupboard items—from dried herbs, tubes of tomato paste and mayonnaise, nuts and olives, to exotic canned fruits, vegetables and hors d'oeuvres—he will also find high quality fresh foods (pâtés and smoked fish, salami sausages and other cooked meats, freshly prepared pasta, salads, cheese and coffee)—the wherewithall to produce an excellent meal with minimum work involved whether it be a candlelight occasion or picnic outing.

Picnics

Pastry is excellent for picnics: pies, pasties, quiches and flans. The time-honoured cold favourites all travel well: lamb cutlets, chicken joints, sliced cold meat, sausages, hard-boiled eggs and cheese. Sandwich fillings should be as moist as possible (for example, tuna fish or cooked chopped chicken should be mixed with mayonnaise and capers); and the fillings should be as thick as one of the slices of bread. Wholemeal and rye bread plus different types of rolls all make a welcome change from plain white sliced bread.

Open sandwiches can be made on the spot, taking butter and a variety of toppings ready prepared in plastic containers. These provide a less stodgy meal than the traditional sandwich and look far more appetizing when combined with salad vegetables. Freshly washed salads and fruits can be drained and packed into airtight containers with tightly fitting lids to keep them crisp and cool.

Also available in the shops are fibreglass insulated packs which will keep foods hot or cold, but any space surrounding the food should be packed with newspaper to prevent loss of temperature. You can also buy sachets for use in the insulated packs; heated in boiling water or frozen in the refrigerator they help to maintain temperature even longer.

Last of all, do not forget to pack cups, plates, knives, forks, spoons, salt, pepper and mustard, sugar and milk in small containers, a can-and-bottle opener—and a damp cloth!

SEASONAL MENUS

Spring

Tuna Stuffed Lemons
Grilled Mackerel with Gooseberry
  Sauce
Apricot Cinnamon Crumble

Avocado Mousse
Spiced Chicken
Caramelized Peaches and Pears

Smoked Salmon Mousse
Duck with Turnips
Treacle Tart

Summer

Salmon Loaf
Chicken in Cider
Fresh Lemon Jelly

Greek Island Salad
Sole with Cream and Iced Grapes
Lemon Soufflé Omelette Flambé

Guacamole
Poached Trout with Herbs
Coeurs à la Crème

Autumn

Courgettes à la Grecque
Casserole of Rabbit
Pineapple Waffles

Smoked Fish Pâté
Veal Marengo
Lemon Sponge Pudding

Fried Whitebait
Fruited Partridge
Cream Cup

Winter

French Onion Soup
Duck with Cherry Sauce
Figs in Pernod

Leek, Onion and Potato Soup
Spiced Mutton Pie
Pears in Chocolate Sauce

Avocado and Seafood Salad
Pheasant in Red Wine
Treacle Tart

RECIPE INDEX